# A PREFACE TO
# EIGHTEENTH CENTURY
# POETRY

# A PREFACE TO
# EIGHTEENTH CENTURY
# POETRY

BY

JAMES SUTHERLAND

OXFORD
AT THE CLARENDON PRESS

*Oxford University Press, Ely House, London W. 1*

GLASGOW NEW YORK TORONTO MELBOURNE WELLINGTON
CAPE TOWN SALISBURY IBADAN NAIROBI DAR ES SALAAM LUSAKA ADDIS ABABA
BOMBAY CALCUTTA MADRAS KARACHI LAHORE DACCA
KUALA LUMPUR SINGAPORE HONG KONG TOKYO

FIRST PUBLISHED 1948
REPRINTED LITHOGRAPHICALLY IN GREAT BRITAIN
AT THE UNIVERSITY PRESS, OXFORD
BY VIVIAN RIDLER
PRINTER TO THE UNIVERSITY
FROM CORRECTED SHEETS OF THE FIRST EDITION
1950, 1958, 1962, 1970

# PREFACE

IN offering to the public of 1798 a volume called *Lyrical Ballads, With a Few Other Poems*, Wordsworth appealed to prospective readers not to approach it with their minds already made up about the sort of pleasure they ought to receive: if they did, they would almost certainly be disappointed. Let them rather try to forget the sort of poetry to which they were accustomed; it was not the only kind:

It is desirable that such readers, for their own sakes, should not suffer the solitary word poetry, a word of very disputed meaning, to stand in the way of their gratification; but that . . . they should consent to be pleased in spite of that most dreadful enemy to our pleasures, our own pre-established codes of decision.

Wise and temperate words, which I gladly appropriate here on behalf of that very poetry against which Wordsworth was warning the reader of 1798. It is, in fact, with pre-established codes of decision, in so far as they obstruct the modern reader's enjoyment of eighteenth-century poetry, that this book is chiefly concerned.

Readers are not to be argued into enjoyment. I hope that I have not made the mistake which Pope attributed to Dennis of trying to 'instruct the Town to dislike what has pleased them, and to be pleased with what they disliked'. I have tried, however, to remove some of the obstacles which impede the modern reader's enjoyment of eighteenth-century poetry, by indicating what the poets were doing and what they were not attempting to do, and by considering why their poetry often differs so sharply from that of other periods. With one or two notable exceptions, few modern critics (it seems to me) have written about eighteenth-century poetry with their eye fixed steadily on the object, or even with any apparent eagerness to study it. To those who have written at large on English poetry, the hundred years from the death of Dryden to the publication of *Lyrical Ballads* have usually appeared as a rather dull plain lying between two ranges of Delectable Mountains, to be hurried across with all convenient speed. Even those who have made a more special study of the period have too often reserved their praise for what is least characteristic of it. Their eyes have been fixed continually on the horizon; and any faint glimmerings of pre-romanticism have been extolled at the expense of the more characteristic and central achievements of the century. It is with these last that I have wished to deal, although in a final chapter some attention is given to those poets who, in one way or another, were unwilling to conform to the standards of the age.

Mr. Norman Callan was kind enough to read the book in manuscript, and I am indebted to him for advice on a number of points. While I was passing the page proofs of the first impression I was able to take advantage of some last-minute comments by Professor D. Nichol Smith, whose generous and unfailing interest in the work of his old students it is a pleasure to record. I should like, too, to record my obligations to those students, in London and Harvard, who listened to the lectures on which this book is based, and who helped me by their agreement or dissent, their encouragement and criticism, to

form with plastic care
Each growing lump, and bring it to a bear.

J. R. S.

# CONTENTS

# ABBREVIATIONS

THE following abbreviations have been used in the footnotes:

| | |
|---|---|
| *Biographia Literaria.* | S. T. Coleridge, *Biographia Literaria,* ed. J. Shawcross, 2 vols. 1907. |
| Boswell, *Life.* | *Boswell's Life of Johnson,* ed. G. B. Hill and L. F. Powell, 4 vols. 1934. |
| Chalmers. | *The Works of the English Poets,* 21 vols. 1810. |
| Dennis, *Critical Works.* | *The Critical Works of John Dennis,* ed. Edward Niles Hooker, 2 vols. 1939–43. |
| Dryden, *Essays.* | *Essays of John Dryden,* ed. W. P. Ker, 2 vols. 1900. |
| Gray, *Correspondence.* | *Correspondence of Thomas Gray,* ed. Paget Toynbee and Leonard Whibley, 3 vols. 1935. |
| Hobbes, *Leviathan.* | 'Everyman' edition. |
| Johnson, *Lives.* | *Lives of the English Poets,* ed. G. B. Hill, 3 vols. 1905. |
| Reynolds, *Discourses.* | 'Everyman' edition. |
| Shaftesbury, *Characteristics.* | *Characteristics of Men, Manners, Opinions, Times,* ed. 1757. |
| Spence, *Anecdotes.* | Joseph Spence, *Anecdotes, Observations, and Characters,* ed. S. W. Singer, 1820. |
| Spingarn. | *Critical Essays of the Seventeenth Century,* ed. J. E. Spingarn, 3 vols. 1908. |
| *S.P.* | *Studies in Philology.* |
| *Wordsworth's Literary Criticism.* | Ed. Nowell C. Smith, 1905. |

# I

## THE BACKGROUND (1)

### I

FOR the study of English poetry in the eighteenth century there is no virtue in taking 1701 as a starting-point: a better date is 1660. On 25 May of that year Samuel Pepys, sitting in a small boat with Mr. Mansell, and one of the King's footmen, and a dog that the King loved, watched Charles II step ashore at Dover, to be greeted by General Monk with all imaginable love and respect, and by a great gathering of noblemen and citizens of all sorts. Four days later, on his birthday, the King entered London ('all things there very gallant and joyful'), and a new page in English history had been turned. The seventeenth century had still forty years to run; but we know now that the church bells that were ringing Charles II into London were ringing in a new age. In the country districts the change was gradual; in London it was rapid and decisive. The need to rebuild the greater part of the City after the Great Fire must have played a considerable part in that modernizing of life which was now taking place, and equally important were the new fashions and the new modes of thought which Charles and his courtiers brought to England from abroad. Many of the ideas which were to dominate the thought of the eighteenth century were not yet in general circulation. Hobbes's *Leviathan* had appeared in 1651; but Newton's *Principia* was not published till 1687, nor Locke's *Essay concerning Human Understanding* till 1690. But the wind had shifted, or was shifting; and poetry, always sensitive to such changes, had begun to feel it almost at once.

### II

This transformation of what it is now fashionable to call the intellectual climate of the age was not simply a shift to a more rationalistic outlook, but it was mainly that. It is pretty generally assumed that this was a change inimical to poetry. Yet the new atmosphere did not make it impossible or even difficult for poets to write; it only made the writing of some kinds of poetry less easy. Hobbes and Locke and many of their contemporaries were subjecting the intellectual atmosphere to a sort of air-conditioning process; the air now being breathed was purer, but it was thinner, and less charged with wandering scents and sounds.

One result of the growing rationalism of the last decades of the seventeenth century was the disappearance from poetry of all that may be comprehensively labelled the supernatural. Looking back across the hundred years that separated him from the Restoration period, Richard Hurd saw clearly what had been happening to poetry. The imagination that had once roved at will 'was now constrained . . . to ally herself with strict truth, if she would gain admittance into reasonable company'. Weighing the gains against the losses, he concluded: 'What we have gotten by this revolution, you will say, is a great deal of good sense. What we have lost, is a world of fine fabling.'[1]

In England, the writer who did more than any other to establish the ascendancy of reason was Thomas Hobbes. Not only did he give reason a new prestige in the scheme of things, but he never missed an opportunity to cast doubt or contempt on any form of mental activity that was not strictly rational. His emphasis on rational thinking was all the more effective because he tended to assume that it was characteristic of the modern mind, and that superstition and credulity belonged to past ages. Hobbes in fact was busy—no one was ever busier— emptying 'the haunted air and gnomed mine', giving rational explanations of phenomena that had once been attributed to gods or daemons. It was for this that he was praised by one of his contemporaries:

> While in dark ignorance we lay, afraid
> Of fancies, ghosts, and every empty shade;
> Great Hobbes appear'd, and by plain Reason's light
> Put such fantastick forms to shameful flight.[2]

In former times, as Hobbes himself pointed out, 'a God, or Divel' had been used to explain 'the nature of powers invisible'. Fawns and nymphs, Lares and genii, ghosts and Furies, fairies and bugbears had all been invented to account for natural phenomena and mental aberrations. Men had 'invoked also their own wit, by the name of *Muses*; their own ignorance, by the name of *Fortune*; their own lust, by the name of *Cupid*; their

---

[1] *Letters on Chivalry and Romance*, ed. Edith J. Morley, p. 154.
[2] John Sheffield, Duke of Buckinghamshire, 'On Mr. Hobbes and his Writings' (Chalmers, x. 97).

own rage, by the name of *Furies*; . . . insomuch as there was nothing, which a poet could introduce as a person in his poem, which they did not make either a *God*, or a *Divel'*.[1] But all that superstitious lumber had gone down the stream of time; men were no longer living in an intellectual twilight, but in the broad light of day. To go against Mr. Hobbes, therefore, was to defend the irrational and to perpetuate the old poetic paraphernalia; you stamped yourself as superstitious and old-fashioned.

As if this were not enough, Hobbes at times came near to equating the imagination with madness. The only kind of mental activity that he really respected was that in which he could observe '*steddy direction* to some approved end'. Without this necessary purposiveness, thinking might easily degenerate into mere mind-wandering or worse. 'But without steddinesse, and direction to some end, a great fancy is one kind of mad-nesse; such as they have, that entring into any discourse, are snatched from their purpose, by every thing that comes in their thought. . . .'[2] If madness might seem to some people too strong to apply to loose and unguided thinking, Hobbes was willing to compare it to day-dreaming. Dreaming itself was another form of mind-wandering ('Waking I often observe the absurdity of dreames'); and from dreams, too, 'did arise the greatest part of the religion of the Gentiles in time past, that worshipped satyres, fawnes, nymphs, and the like; and now adayes the opinion that rude people have of fayries, ghosts, and goblins; and of the power of witches'.[3] It was only 'rude people', it will be noticed, who still believed in witches and fairies. Such notions belonged to the childhood of a race; but when a nation had intellectually come of age it put away childish things.

In his attitude to the child and to childish ideas Hobbes was in no sense peculiar, even though he was a bachelor and getting on to sixty when he was writing his *Leviathan*. The glorification of the child is a romantic habit. The eighteenth century gener-ally thought of the child as an undeveloped adult, a half-articulate being which might come to full intellectual stature when it grew up, but which was not yet fully developed men-tally and was therefore of only limited interest. Poets such as Ambrose Philips, who constituted himself a sort of unofficial

[1] *Leviathan*, p. 57.　　　　[2] Ibid., p. 33.
[3] Ibid., pp. 6, 7.

laureate of children, only incurred ridicule. In 'The Art of
Sinking in Poetry' Pope laughed at his 'infantine' style, and it
was of course for this vein of poetry that Philips acquired the
nickname of 'Namby-Pamby'. If you wanted to write about
children Matthew Prior had already shown in his 'Letter to
the Honourable Lady Miss Margaret-Cavendish-Holles-Harley'
how it could be done without losing your self-respect:

> My noble, lovely, little Peggy,
> Let this, my first-epistle, beg ye,
> At dawn of morn, and close of even,
> To lift your heart and hands to heaven:
> In double beauty say your pray'r,
> Our father first, then notre père. . . .[1]

But then Prior had the perfect poise of the assured artist; he
knew just how far to go, and just how serious he ought to be if
he was to please the noble parents of little Peggy and yet not
incur the ridicule of that much larger public who were not her
parents.

To Hobbes, then, the right man was the adult, the man who
was living in the clear light of reason, who had stepped free
from all superstition, and who could think steadily—controlling
alike his imagination and his prejudice. Had he gone so far as
to sneer openly at the imagination, he might have found an
opponent with the courage and the ability to answer him; but
he did something subtler and far more damaging—he simply
assumed that it was most commonly to be found in children,
lunatics, and the uneducated.[2]

The work of making men aware of their own mental pro-
cesses was carried farther by John Locke in his *Essay concerning
Human Understanding*. Locke steadily cleared away the jungle in
which had lurked the unknown and mysterious and terrifying
creatures of the imagination; he let in the light of reason, and
others were soon ploughing and sowing in what had once been
unexplored and dangerous country. Among those others was
Addison. Anything that Addison wrote in a *Tatler* or a *Spectator* was probably repeated, with individual modifications, by
hundreds of sensible Londoners in the course of the following
week, and from them it spread outwards and downwards to
many thousands more. It is therefore of some significance in
the history of ideas that Addison, a confessed admirer of Locke,

---

[1] Chalmers, x. 243 f.    [2] See Note A, p. 168.

should have given a good deal of his space to ridiculing or otherwise discountenancing witchcraft, ghosts, premonitions, omens, and superstitions of all kinds, and that he should have done much to popularize Locke's rational explanation of the working of the human mind. On 6 July 1711 he told the readers of the *Spectator* what Locke in his chapter on the association of ideas had to say about goblins and sprites, the topic being introduced by way of one of Sir Roger's footmen who, coming past the ruins of an old abbey at night, 'had been almost frighted out of his wits by a spirit that appeared to him in the shape of a black horse without an head'. Mr. Spectator, ignoring the butler's warning, walked that way at dusk himself: 'I observed a cow grazing not far from me, which an imagination that was apt to startle might easily have construed into a black horse without an head: and I dare say the poor footman lost his wits upon some such trivial occasion.' A week later (14 July) Mr. Spectator was discussing the question: Are there such creatures as witches? With characteristic tact Addison pronounces his opinion: 'I believe in general that there is, and has been such a thing as witchcraft; but at the same time can give no credit to any particular instance of it.' That was about as far as Addison could safely carry his public in 1711. Yet in his account of Moll White, a reputed witch, he tried to ridicule the whole idea of witchcraft. Sir Roger (he tells us) was in two minds about her: when he visited the old woman in her wretched cottage he winked to Mr. Spectator and pointed to an old broom-staff behind the door, but he advised Moll, as a justice of peace, 'to avoid all communication with the devil, and never to hurt any of her neighbour's cattle'. Left to himself, indeed, Sir Roger would on several occasions have bound the old woman over to the county sessions for 'making children spit pins, and giving maids the nightmare', but he had been dissuaded by his chaplain. The essay closes on a more serious note:

I have been the more particular in this account, because I hear there is scarce a village in England that has not a Moll White in it. When an old woman begins to doat, and grow chargeable to a parish, she is generally turned into a witch, and fills the whole country with extravagant fancies, imaginary distempers, and terrifying dreams. In the mean time, the poor wretch that is the innocent occasion of so many evils, begins to be frighted at herself, and sometimes confesses secret commerces and familiarities that her imagination forms in a delirious old age. This frequently cuts off charity from the greatest objects of compassion, and inspires people with a malevolence towards those poor decrepit parts of our species, in whom human nature is defaced by infirmity and dotage.

Perhaps we are too ready to sneer at Addison; the work he did was often more necessary than we always realize to-day. On 18 January 1700, for instance, the readers of the *Post-Boy* were given a ghastly account of how an old woman, supposed to be a witch, was done to death by a rabble at St. Albans.

*London,* Jan. 18.

We are inform'd from St. Albans, that one Amey Townsend, who lay under the misfortune of being a reputed witch, about ten days since going by a watchmaker's shop in that corporation, ask'd the price of a watch; the apprentice snapt her up short, saying, What's that to you, forty shillings is more than you are worth; upon which 'twas observ'd, that she only pointed at the boy with her finger, and trudg'd about her business. Her character struck the lad with such frightful apprehensions of danger from the reputed hagg, that next day he fell sick in good earnest; keeps his bed, cries out, Amey Townsend had bewitch'd him, and he should dye, if he did not immediately fetch blood from her. The poor old creature was brought in the lad's chamber, he, in a great fury, leaps out of bed, sets his nails in her face, made her bleed, and the boy recovered, while the poor wretch was turn'd out of doors to seek her remedy for being severely scratch'd. The mob learnedly debating this affair, concluded that the boy was bewitch'd by Townsend, and they in justice ought to inflict the punishment by making an experiment. Immediately they seize the poor soul, force her into a river near the town, and drag her so often through it, till she was like to expire by their barbarous usage: which some of the brutes perceiving, had the humanity to put her into a warm bed, where she lay in a hopeful way of recovery. Some of the more judicious inhabitants discanting upon her being duck'd, averr'd they saw her swim, ergo, she was a witch, and scandalous to that corporation. This further enrages the mob (who always are bewitch'd and tumultuous), they assemble again in a body, haul the miserable creature out of her bed, and setting her in a chair, hoist her upon their shoulders, and carried her about the town in triumph, shouting and bauling out *a Townsend, a Townsend*: after which they had her before a justice of the peace, who to appease them, sent her to the town-house, where she died in two hours. And we hear that several are taken up to answer it at the next assizes for Hertfordshire, where no question but some of them will decently swing for it.

The Romantic poets of the nineteenth century, separated by a comfortable gap of time from such hideous outbieaks of superstition, could afford to toy happily with demonology and witchcraft, and were not above reproaching the eighteenth century for its rationalism. But the eighteenth century had been too recently delivered from a genuine belief in witchcraft and similar occult phenomena to encourage any 'willing suspension of disbelief' of this kind among its poets. It held, precariously enough, to its newly won sanity.

Hobbes and Locke come closer to the poet's business in their distinction between fancy (or imagination) and judgement. Though he went so far as to admit that in good poems Fancy was more prominent than Judgement because 'they please for the extravagancy',[1] Hobbes yet insisted that the Fancy should be always under control. So long as the poet's thoughts were applied to some end clearly foreseen and consistently pursued, Hobbes was ready enough to welcome imagination in a poet; but its main function, in his opinion, was to provide the poet with similes and metaphors and so enable him to illustrate his thoughts delightfully. He would have approved Dryden's well-known simile for the imaginative faculty in the writer, 'which, like a nimble spaniel, beats over and ranges through the field of memory, till it springs the quarry it hunted after'.[2] He would have approved because the simile seems to have originated in a remark of his own.[3] This Hobbes–Dryden spaniel is not ranging aimlessly, but pursuing a scent which will lead him at last to the game he is seeking. What Hobbes did not approve was the untrained mongrel who raced backwards and forwards across the field, aimless and yelping. Mere mind-wandering in an author, or the complete abandonment of the mind to the emotions, would never lead to a great poem. As Johnson once said to Sir Joshua Reynolds about Macpherson's *Ossian*: 'Sir, a man might write such stuff for ever, if he would *abandon* his mind to it.'[4]

To Hobbes, again, 'wit' and 'judgement' appeared as two opposed forces: wit was only too apt to gallop away with good sense, and it was the business of the judgement to curb its extravagance. The necessary antagonism of wit and judgement

[1] *Leviathan*, p. 34.
[2] Preface to *Annus Mirabilis*, *Essays*, i. 14.
[3] *Leviathan*, p. 10.                    [4] Boswell, *Life*, iii. 183.

became a critical commonplace of the period. Writing of the poetry of the Arabians, Thomas Rymer asserted (1674):

> Fancy with them is predominant, is wild, vast, and unbridled, o're which their *judgement* has little command or authority: hence their conceptions are monstrous, and have nothing of exactness, nothing of resemblance or proportion.[1]

And Pope's well-known lines in the *Essay on Criticism* repeat the customary antithesis:

> Some, to whom Heav'n in wit has been profuse,
> Want as much more, to turn it to its use;
> For wit and judgment often are at strife,
> Tho' meant each other's aid, like man and wife.[2]

This new distrust of 'wit'—a distrust of the free, spontaneous association of ideas as contrasted with the more sober progress of the thoughts under 'steddy direction to some approved end' —is no doubt responsible for the disappointment felt by some readers of eighteenth-century poetry. In poetry there must always be a compromise between the foreseen and the fortuitous, between the deliberate and the spontaneous. The poet (unless he is writing a 'Kubla Khan') knows where he is going, but he does not necessarily know every point that he will pass on his way. Where nothing at all is foreseen and everything is left to the inspiration of the moment, the result is more likely to be a poetic phantasmagoria[3] than a poem; the reader will probably feel a lack of movement and direction. Where, how-ever, everything, or too much, is foreseen, his mind may be improved but it is less likely to be excited; he may admire the flawless intellectual structure, but he is likely to be oppressed by a sense of too complete deliberation. Much eighteenth-century poetry is the poetry of calm and measured statement. 'The hardest thing in the world', it was observed by one of the most judicious of Dryden's contemporaries, 'is to give the thoughts due liberty and yet retain them in due discipline.'[4] What is accepted as *due* liberty differs from one age to another. If the Romantic poets were ready to risk much, and those of the twentieth century to chance almost everything, for the

---

[1] Spingarn, ii. 165.      [2] ll. 80 ff.

[3] 'A shifting series or succession of phantasms or imaginary figures, as seen in a dream or fevered condition, [or] as called up by the imagination . . .' (*O.E.D.*).

[4] *The Life and Letters of Sir George Savile, Bart., First Marquis of Halifax*, ed. H. C. Foxcroft, 1898, ii. 523.

mind's liberty to roam, most modern readers will probably feel that the poets of the eighteenth century were too much inclined to emphasize the 'due discipline'. They have had to pay for it in an age in which poetry is often equated with the irrational, or in which at least the reason is looked upon as nothing better than a necessary alloy in poetry. It is never easy to realize that the poetry of one's own contemporaries is only the latest fashion; it is fatally easy to assume (as the eighteenth century certainly did) that we have advanced beyond earlier generations, if not in actual performance, then at least in our understanding of what poetry is. In reality we have only fused the elements together in different proportions. In eighteenth-century poetry the proportion of Reason to the Irrational was perhaps 3 : 2, or more; in the poetry of Yeats, Eliot, or Dylan Thomas the proportions are often reversed. We must accept the difference, and resist the temptation to grade the poetical production of the two centuries by reference to our own private formula for poetry.

III

An age which was becoming increasingly interested in science was naturally attracted to that kind of truth which is universal and demonstrable. Conversely, it tended to view with increasing suspicion that sort of thought which was merely personal, or, worse still, peculiar. More and more the age interested itself in the usual, the 'natural', the event that could be counted upon to recur, the thoughts and feelings that were shared by all normal people and that had therefore a general validity. That was the theory, at any rate, though in practice the age of Hobbes and Locke, and later of Addison and of Johnson, was only too ready to dismiss as unnatural any thought or feeling which lay outside the range of its experience, or which was markedly different from what had become customary. But the dislike of the peculiar or the abnormal was real enough; and in its widest manifestations it must be related to a new desire for that general truth in which the man of science deals. Among readers of poetry it took the form of a sharp reaction against the work of the Metaphysical poets, which a new generation had begun to find hopelessly odd and unnatural, and which was quite out of fashion by 1700.

What the eighteenth century thought of the metaphysical

B

poets is fully set forth in Johnson's 'Life of Cowley'. He objects to them on several counts, but the weight of his indictment rests on the charge that they continually sought for the unexpected and the surprising, and paid far too little attention to that 'uniformity of sentiment' which enables a writer to understand and express the thoughts and feelings of all normal men. So eccentric was their mode of thinking that they could hardly be said to partake of human nature at all: a visitor from Mars might think like them, but hardly an inhabitant of this earth. In their poetry, Johnson felt, they did not copy either nature or life; they did not represent 'the operations of intellect' (i.e. the way that normal human beings think). They were therefore, in the most damaging sense, unrepresentative of the human race; and in consequence what they had to say could have little importance.

Johnson has been quoted here because he gives the fullest and most reasoned statement of the eighteenth-century case against the Metaphysicals; but the reaction against them had set in long before the close of the seventeenth century. The modern reader who is ready to be impatient with some of the points that Johnson makes would do well to consider them, not in relation to Donne, but to Cowley, or, better still, Cleveland. Johnson contents himself with one quotation from Cleveland, but it illustrates well the sort of odd, unnatural, and barely human utterance of which he complains:

> Since 'tis my doom, love's undershrieve,
> Why this reprieve?
> Why doth my she-advowson fly
> Incumbency? . . .
> To sell thyself dost thou intend
> By candle end?
> And hold the contract thus in doubt,
> Life's taper out?
> Think but how soon the market fails;
> Your sex lives faster than the males;
> As if, to measure age's span,
> The sober Julian were th' account of man,
> Whilst you live by the fleet Gregorian.

'Who', Johnson asks, 'would imagine it possible that in a very few lines so many remote ideas could be brought together?'[1]

[1] *Lives*, i. 27.

Cleveland's poem ('To Julia to expedite her Promise') and Herrick's 'Gather ye rosebuds' are variations on a similar theme; but in Herrick's poem the eighteenth-century reader would have recognized a normal poetic argument (Time is never at a standstill; the flowers fade all too soon; the higher the sun climbs, the sooner his journey will be over and night must fall. So, too, youth must yield to age; therefore, maidens, 'use your time, and while ye may, goe marry'.) In Cleveland's poem he would have felt that nothing was natural, that no man but Cleveland had ever thought like that (cf. Johnson's 'Who but Donne would have thought that a good man is a telescope?'),[1] and that therefore the poem lacked the sanction which is given to poetry that expresses the common sense of mankind.

The very marked reaction from the Metaphysical poets is part of a wider movement of the human mind. But that aspect of the reaction which had its origin in a dislike of the eccentric and the peculiar, and of what may be called private thoughts and private feelings, may become more intelligible if it is related to the religious history of the period. The seventeenth century in England had proved a fertile ground for the growth of religious sects, most of which came into being because some individual had seen an inner light. Of this kind were the Muggletonians, who take their name from their founder, Lodowicke Muggleton (1609–98). Muggleton had inward revelations, and suffered the usual punishments of being fined, pilloried, and imprisoned; but he was only one (and one of the most sensible) of many such fanatics or 'enthusiasts' who claimed to be inspired. On 24 October 1656, on a day of torrential rain, James Nayler, who claimed that 'Christ was in him', rode into Bristol, surrounded by his disciples and followers crying, 'Holy, holy, holy, Lord God of Israel.' For this he was pilloried, whipped, and branded on the forehead. Such individuals may, of course, appear at any time, and were, in fact, to appear again in the eighteenth century; but the spiritual climate of the seventeenth century seems to have been particularly favourable to their growth. In spite of harsh persecution they flourished, and each new Messiah gathered round him a body of fanatical followers, who, as often as not, proceeded to split up into secondary schisms as new 'voices' were heard or new visions vouchsafed.

[1] Ibid., p. 26.

At the very beginning of the eighteenth century, only a few years before the *Tatler* and the *Spectator* were to reflect in their pages an England that now appears to us wonderfully stable, a fresh outbreak of fanaticism was alarming the more reasonable subjects of Queen Anne. A group of Camisars, known as the French Prophets, had come to London, and their predictions of strange and terrible events were frightening the simple-minded and amusing the more sophisticated. Moved by odd physical agitations, they would break out suddenly into prophetical utterance: fire and brimstone were to pour down upon London, a boat was to sail along the streets in the blood of the slain, and Lord Chief Justice Holt (who had sentenced some of the prophets to the pillory) was to die horribly even as he sat on the bench, the blood bursting out of his veins from head to feet. Soon the French Prophets had attracted several hundreds of English followers, and an Englishman, John Lacy, became the acknowledged leader of the movement. One of his brother prophets rashly foretold how he would raise one of their brethren from the dead; and on the day appointed for this miracle two regiments of train-bands had to be called out to keep order around Bunhill Fields burying-ground, where the dead man lay buried. Lacy prudently called off the miracle. Later a revelation came to him that he must put away his wife and take to his bed a prophetess, Elizabeth Gray, on whom he would beget a second Messiah. Lacy obeyed the voice of the Spirit, and Elizabeth Gray was brought to bed of a daughter. A year or two more, and it was all over; the Prophets had scattered, leaving only some startling memories and a mass of prophetical writings in print.[1]

It is against such a background that we must view the eighteenth century's distrust of inspiration. The word itself was in low repute for the greater part of the century, and was used on most occasions to describe that kind of private illumination (the 'inner light') which came to religious impostors and fanatics. So, too, the word 'enthusiasm' had generally the meaning given to it in Johnson's *Dictionary*: 'a vain confidence of divine favour or communication'. Rising majestically above this undignified hubbub of fanaticism was the solid edifice of the Church of England, the right place of worship for sensible

[1] I have given an account of John Lacy in *Background for Queen Anne*, 1939, pp. 36–74.

Englishmen. 'For my part,' said one of them,[1] 'I admire it chiefly for this reason, that it is fit for the people, subject to the laws, and most suitable to the clergy. For here, without care, without thought, and without trouble, honour and ease are enjoyed at once, which is a state that most men wish for.' That is not quite how Swift would have put it; but in *A Tale of a Tub* and in *The Mechanical Operation of the Spirit* he satirizes fanaticism and false claims to inspiration. In a *Letter concerning Enthusiasm* (1707) Shaftesbury, with Lacy and his brother prophets in mind, recommends raillery and good humour as the best answer to those who claim a private religious inspiration or revelation. The verdict of one of Lacy's contemporaries sums up the attitude of the average eighteenth-century bystander to such manifestations of religious enthusiasm:

That which I think comes nearest to Mr. Lacy's case, is a more than ordinary vanity and ambition of being thought wiser and better than the rest of the world, which, join'd with an affectation of singularity, and having the glory of starting something that's odd and out of the way, and being the originals of his own opinion, which he thinks is an infallible proof that the reach of his own understanding is above the common standard, is turn'd at length to subtlety and artifice, to doubling and insincerity, to deceive and being deceived.[2]

The hostility which Wesley and Whitfield aroused in the 1740s when the Methodist movement was spreading through the poorer classes of society is to be attributed in part, no doubt, to the natural dislike of the easy-going for anyone who sets himself up to be better than other people, but partly to a fear that the old fanaticism was coming back, and that the established order was once more being called to question. Englishmen had had enough of intellectual adventure. Wesley and his followers might feel themselves driven by some inner compulsion to travel towards the celestial city,

> And nightly pitch their moving tents
> A day's march nearer home.

But in the 1740s most Englishmen asked nothing better than to be allowed to sleep quietly in their beds.

That the more critical minds of the period perceived some

[1] Sir Godfrey Copley; cited by Walter Wilson, *Memoirs of the Life and Times of Daniel De Foe*, ii. 132.
[2] Richard Kingston, *Enthusiastick Impostors*, 1707; cited in *Background for Queen Anne*, p. 74.

connexion between the claims of an individual to be religiously inspired and the claims of a poet to poetical inspiration may be deduced from Shaftesbury's *Letter concerning Enthusiasm*, or, better still, from Dryden's dry humour at the expense of Elkanah Settle:

Mr. Settle having never studied any sort of learning but poetry, and that but slenderly, as you may find by his writings, and having besides no other advantages, must make very lame work on 't; he himself declares, he neither reads nor cares for conversation; so that he would persuade us he is a kind of fanatic in poetry, and has a light within him, and writes by an inspiration; which (like that of the heathen prophets) a man must have no sense of his own when he receives; and no doubt he would be thought inspired, and would be reverenced extremely in the country where Santons are worshipped.[1]

One of Dryden's contemporaries similarly warns the poet against false inspiration:

> Beware *what spirit* rages in your breast;
> For ten inspir'd ten thousand are possest.[2]

Here again the issue involved the rival claims of Reason and Fancy to dominate men's minds. And the significance of this conflict lay in the fact that you could hope for general agreement among thinking people, because truth—the one inevitable and unchanging truth—was waiting to be apprehended by those who used their reason; whereas if men were foolish enough to trust to their fancy, you might have a hundred different notions, each one as good as the next. As Rymer put it:

A poet is not to leave his reason, and blindly abandon himself to follow fancy, for then his fancy might be monstrous, might be singular, and please no body's maggot but his own; but reason is to be his guide, reason is common to all people, and can never carry him from what is natural.[3]

By 'reason is common to all people' Rymer does not mean, of course, that all men are reasonable; indeed, no one was more ready than he to emphasize the unreasonableness of the mob, and to contrast the unthinking 'people' with 'the wise'. He does mean that if only men can be persuaded to use their reason they will all arrive at the same point—the point, in fact, where truth is to be found. And this truth is identical with

---

[1] *Works*, ed. Sir Walter Scott, 1808, xv. 411.
[2] Roscommon, 'Essay on Translated Verse', Spingarn, ii. 306. See Note B, p. 168.
[3] Spingarn, ii. 192.

Nature; and since it is attainable by the rational faculties of man it is necessarily 'what oft was thought'.

If the Metaphysicals were out of fashion because they were too odd and 'unnatural', Shakespeare and many other Elizabethan poets also disappointed the new desire for what oft was thought by being too rich and metaphorical. The changed outlook becomes apparent if we examine the kind of alterations made by Dryden when re-tailoring Shakespeare for the Restoration stage. One of his first tasks was to chip off most of the metaphorical incrustation so as to allow the thought to appear to an English audience in the 1670s and 1680s. In his version of *Troilus and Cressida* he gets to work early with a speech of Troilus (1. i. 44):

> Oh Pandarus! I tell thee Pandarus—
> When I doe tell thee, there my hopes lye drown'd:
> Reply not in how many fadomes deepe
> They lye indrench'd. I tell thee, I am mad
> In Cressid's love. Thou answer'st she is faire,
> Powr'st in the open ulcer of my heart,
> Her eyes, her haire, her cheeke, her gate, her voice;
> Handlest in thy discourse, O, that her hand,
> In whose comparison, all whites are inke,
> Writing their owne reproach; to whose soft seizure,
> The cignet's downe is harsh, and spirit of sense
> Hard as the palme of plough-man. This thou tel'st me;
> As true thou tel'st me when I say I love her:
> But saying thus, instead of oyle and balme,
> Thou lai'st in every gash that love hath given me,
> The knife that made it.

For this Dryden substitutes something at once simpler and briefer:

> Oh Pandarus, when I tell thee I am mad
> In Cressid's love, thou answer'st she is fair;
> Praisest her eyes, her stature, and her wit;
> But praising thus, instead of oil and balm,
> Thou lay'st, in every wound her love has given me,
> The sword that made it.

Of Shakespeare's rich cargo of metaphor Dryden jettisons everything but oil and balm, wound and sword. ('Sword' for 'knife', because knife was a 'mean' expression.) He retains, in fact, only the easiest (because the most obvious) metaphor, and so brings the passage closer to the language of discourse. Wounds given to the lover by his mistress belonged to the common stock of poetical metaphor; and oil and balm poured in the wound were hardly less familiar. The 'turn' given to the thought by laying the sword in the very wound it has made was the sort of wit the Restoration audience was well fitted to understand and enjoy. So Dryden keeps that. But taken undiluted, Shakespeare was altogether too strong for the Restoration palate. If in this new age poetry was not going to be written in basic English, the contemporary distaste for excess, extravagance, caprice, obscurity, was to bring it at times dangerously near to using a sort of basic metaphor. The nineteenth century was to get again (and enjoy) this easy metaphor in the poetry of Byron, by far the most popular of the Romantic poets.

But in the best poets of the eighteenth century—certainly in Pope—the conventional is nicely varied with the unconventional. For poets who are working mainly with conventional imagery the possibilities of the unusual and unexpected are enormous. Many of them deliberately exploited the shock.

> Dorinda's sparkling wit and eyes
>   United cast too fierce a light,
> Which blazes high, but quickly dies,
>   Pains not the heart, but hurts the sight.

> Love is a calmer, gentler joy,
>   Smooth are his looks, and soft his pace,
> Her Cupid is a blackguard boy,
>   That runs his link full in your face.[1]

The first six lines almost bait a trap for us which is sprung in the last two. Pope, particularly in his satires, where denigration gave him a freedom that he did not enjoy so fully in other and more dignified compositions, often delights in jabbing at the reader's sense of propriety with an unusual image:

>                 his soul
> Still sits at squat, and peeps not from its hole.

> Or at the ear of Eve, familiar toad,
> Half froth, half venom, spits himself abroad.

> Nonsense precipitate, like running lead,
> That slip'd thro' cracks and zig-zags of the head.[2]

[1] By Charles Sackville, 6th Earl of Dorset (Chalmers, viii. 345).
[2] *Moral Essays*, i. 55 f.; *Epistle to Dr. Arbuthnot*, ll. 319 f.; *The Dunciad*, i. 123 f.

Such effects sparkle all the more brilliantly from being not too thickly sown. They stand out from a background of more conventional imagery, which, if not the expression of every day, was at least 'how oft it had been put' in poetry, and could therefore be assimilated without too much disturbance of the established habits of association. Outside satire, the poet had less occasion for the startling or unconventional metaphor. His happiest effects, indeed, are often obtained by a sort of apotheosis of the usual, as when Goldsmith tells us how the Parson looked after his little flock with a tender solicitude—

> But all his serious thoughts had rest in Heaven.
> As some tall cliff, that lifts its awful form,
> Swells from the vale, and midway leaves the storm,
> Though round its breast the rolling clouds are spread,
> Eternal sunshine settles on its head.[1]

## IV

The modern reader, with whom the Metaphysical poets are once more in fashion, may not find it easy to sympathize with the eighteenth century's dislike of the peculiar; he is likely to find it even harder to understand its distrust of originality. The word itself is surprisingly recent. The earliest example given by the *Oxford English Dictionary*, meaning 'the quality of being independent of and different from anything that has appeared before', is 1787. The adjective 'original', meaning 'novel or fresh in character or style', is a little earlier, but as applied to persons ('capable of original ideas or actions, inventive, creative') does not seem to go farther back than the beginning of the nineteenth century. Even more significant is the meaning sometimes given to the noun: 'an original' might be a person who acted in an original way, but also one who was *ridiculously* different from other people, 'a singular, odd, or eccentric person' (*O.E.D.*). In Wycherley's *Plain Dealer* (1674) there is a foolish character called Novel, who 'affects novelty as much as the fashion, . . . who likes nothing but what is new'. On his first entrance he boasts of this weakness: 'I must confess I hate imitation, to do any thing like other people. All that know me do me the honour to say, I am an original, faith.'[2] To say of a writer in 1700 that he was 'an original' was almost

---

[1] *The Deserted Village*, ll. 188 ff.     [2] II. i.

certainly to sneer at him: by 1800 the words conveyed high praise—perhaps the highest of all. How did this remarkable change of attitude come about?

One of the clearest statements of the eighteenth century's attitude to originality is to be found in the *Spectator*, 20 December 1711, where Addison is paraphrasing some observations by Boileau:

> Wit and fine writing doth not consist so much in advancing things that are new, as in giving things that are known an agreeable turn. It is impossible for us, who live in the latter ages of the world, to make observations in criticism, morality, or in any art or science, which have not been touched upon by others. We have little else left us, but to represent the common sense of mankind in more strong, more beautiful, or more uncommon lights.

Originality is not entirely ruled out by Addison, but it can be shown only in the treatment of the material. Has it ever been remarked how close Addison's last words come to the better-known passage in *Biographia Literaria* where Coleridge is discussing 'the two cardinal points of poetry, the power of exciting the sympathy of the reader by a faithful adherence to the truth of nature, and the power of giving the interest of novelty by the modifying colours of the imagination'? To illustrate the possibility of combining both, Coleridge refers his reader to 'the sudden charm which accidents of light and shade, which moonlight or sunlight, diffuse over a known and familiar landscape'.[1] This is not very different from Addison's 'more uncommon lights'. But there is, of course, a difference: Addison is thinking mainly in terms of a new treatment of the old thoughts or human situations, and Coleridge is thinking of a new vision, an entirely new experience, of those permanent 'truths of nature'. To Addison, at any rate, it seems quite hopeless to expect many new thoughts, characters, or situations in an eighteenth-century writer; he has come upon the scene too late for that. From Dryden to Johnson this attitude to the past is almost universal. Writing of the Elizabethan and Jacobean dramatists, Dryden bemoans[2] the prodigality with which they spent their wit:

> We acknowledge them our fathers in wit; but they have ruined their estates themselves, before they came to their children's hands.

---

[1] Op. cit. ii. 5.     [2] *Essays*, i. 99.

There is scarce an humour, a character, or any kind of plot, which they have not blown upon. All comes sullied or wasted to us. . . .

Dryden was not always quite so pessimistic as this, but he was expressing an attitude that was already widespread. Some seventy years later an eighteenth-century journalist quotes feelingly the remark made by a French poet on reading a beautiful ode of Horace: 'D——n these ancients (says he) they have stolen all my fine thoughts.'[1]

The equally firm conviction that even if originality were possible it would still be undesirable must be related once again to the belief that poetry was concerned with what oft was thought. Any new thought could only, at this late date, be peculiar or out of the way. As an anonymous journalist writing in 1728 put it:

We cannot applaud a thought but so far as we find it conformable to what nature and our reason have always dictated to us; that is, to what we our selves thought and felt within our selves. Consequently they were the very same thoughts and sentiments which we our selves had before, tho' we did not actually attend to, or reflect upon them.[2]

The eighteenth-century poet was therefore not only a man speaking to men, but a man speaking what all of us had already spoken, or might have spoken if we had been fully conscious of our thoughts. Among eighteenth-century critics no one insisted more frequently than Johnson that poetry deals with the recurring thoughts and feelings of the human race. Gray's *Elegy* is praised because it 'abounds with images which find a mirror in every mind, and with sentiments to which every bosom returns an echo'. Dyer's 'Grongar Hill' is approved because 'the reflections of the writer [are] so consonant to the general sense or experience of mankind'. On the other hand, Collins made the mistake of 'indulging some peculiar habits of thought',[3] and so presumably lost touch with the common reader. To orthodox opinion in the eighteenth century the mere fact that a thing had

---

[1] *Common Sense*, 11 June 1737. The same complaint was made frequently by Johnson; e.g. 'Whatever can happen to man has happened so often, that little remains for fancy and invention' (see Boswell, *Life*, ii. 358, n. 3). But already there were some who rejected this rather defeatist attitude and stressed the need for originality. See especially Edward Young, *Conjectures on Original Composition*, 1759.

[2] *The Flying Post, or Weekly Medley*, 9 Nov. 1728.

[3] *Lives*, iii. 441, 345, 337.

not been said before was almost sufficient to raise a doubt if it was worth saying.

It has been suggested that the advance of Science (and particularly of the mathematical sciences) quickened men's interest in natural laws, and, more generally, in that sort of truth which was universal and above all particular instances. But we ought perhaps to distinguish a directly contrary effect encouraged by the steady advance during the same period of the biological sciences. They, too, it is true, aspire to universal truth and to the formulation of natural laws; but *in practice* they proceed much more by the collection and study of individual instances. At all events, there can be no question that the pioneer work of botanists and zoologists, and even the less integrated activities of the despised virtuosos, were opening men's minds to the extraordinary number of natural objects which had never before been noticed, or, if noticed, never brought to their attention. In one of his *Guardian* essays Steele wrote an enthusiastic review of Derham's *Physico-Theology*. Derham, he said, had revealed 'as with a wand . . . the wonders and spectacles in all nature'; and Steele was prompted by his reading of the book to reflect upon how much Derham had made him see for the first time:

It is a very desirable entertainment to find occasions of pleasure and satisfaction in those objects and occurrences which we have all our lives, perhaps, overlooked; or beheld, without exciting any reflections that made us wiser, or happier.[1]

Here Steele is coming near to commending what oft was *not* thought. It is significant that Johnson praises Thomson's *Seasons* for much the same reason. After remarking that Thomson's mind 'at once comprehends the vast, and attends to the minute', he continues:

The reader of *The Seasons* wonders that he never saw before what Thomson shews him, and that he never yet has felt what Thomson impresses.[2]

Is Johnson inconsistent here? Can his reason for praising Thomson be reconciled with the reasons he gives for commending Gray's *Elegy*? In all probability Johnson made a distinction between the poet who dealt with human life and the poet who

[1] *Guardian*, No. 175, 1 Oct. 1713.                    [2] *Lives*, iii. 299.

was primarily concerned with the description of nature. Man
had been the universal subject of the poets from the time of
Homer onwards; that subject had been fully treated by the
best minds of all ages, and we could not therefore expect to
make many more discoveries *there*. Nature was another matter
altogether: the author of *The Seasons* was not, of course, the
first to deal with that subject, but he was working in a field that
had never been intensely cultivated, and there were still opportunities for him to discover what was at once new and natural.
Johnson would no doubt have liked Thomson less if he had not
comprehended the vast and offered to his readers a 'wide
expansion of general views', but granted that, he was ready to
enjoy the poet's 'enumeration of circumstantial varieties'.

Perhaps the fullest justification of the eighteenth-century
attitude to novelty and singularity is to be found in the Seventh
Discourse of Sir Joshua Reynolds. Our bodies, he says, are
roughly alike: so are our minds. There is 'a general uniformity
and agreement in the minds of men'. If there were not, we
should never have been able to establish the rules of art: unless
we had been able to count on other people thinking and feeling
like ourselves we should never have known how to appeal to
them. But there *is* a general agreement.

We may suppose a uniformity, and conclude that the same effect
will be produced by the same cause in the minds of others. . . . We
can never be sure that our own sensations are true and right, till
they are confirmed by more extensive observation. One man op-
posing another determines nothing; but a general union of minds,
like a general combination of the forces of all mankind, makes a
strength that is irresistible. . . . A man who thinks he is guarding
himself against prejudices by resisting the authority of others, leaves
open every avenue to singularity, vanity, self-conceit, obstinacy, and
many other vices, all tending to warp the judgment, and prevent the
natural operation of his faculties. This submission to others is a
deference which we owe, and indeed are forced involuntarily to pay.
In fact, we are never satisfied with our opinions, whatever we may
pretend, till they are ratified and confirmed by the suffrages of the
rest of mankind. . . .[1]

The firm hold which such ideas had on the minds of most
readers of poetry may be seen from the way in which Francis
Jeffrey reacted to the poetry of Wordsworth. Reviewing

[1] *Discourses*, pp. 116 ff.

Crabbe's *Poems* (1807), Jeffrey showed how much he was still dominated by the ideas of poetry he had formed when he was still a boy. He contrasted Crabbe favourably with Wordsworth and the other 'gentlemen of the new school', who

scarcely ever condescend to take their subjects from any description of persons at all known to the common inhabitants of the world; but invent for themselves certain whimsical and unheard-of beings, to whom they impute some fantastical combination of feelings, and then labour to excite our sympathy for them, either by placing them in incredible situations, or by some strained and exaggerated moralization of a vague and tragical description.

How much better Mr. Crabbe did these things!

Mr. Crabbe, in short, shows us something which we have all seen, or may see, in real life; and draws from it such feelings and such reflections as every human being must acknowledge that it is calculated to excite. . . . Mr. Wordsworth and his associates, on the other hand, introduce us to beings whose existence was not previously suspected by the acutest observers of nature; 'and excite an interest for them—where they do excite any interest—more by an eloquent and refined analysis of their own capricious feelings, than by any obvious or intelligible ground of sympathy in their situation.[1]

If the modern reader is inclined to discount Jeffrey as the last stronghold of outworn critical ideas in a new and more imaginative age, perhaps he will listen more sympathetically to Keats. In a letter to his publisher, dated 27 February 1818, Keats set forth one or two axioms for poetry, and the first of these was that poetry should never surprise by its singularity:

It should strike the reader as a wording of his own highest thoughts, and appear almost a Remembrance.[2]

In view of what Keats had to say about neo-classical poets in his 'Sleep and Poetry' it may seem rash to suggest that he had any sympathies whatever with those who lined up behind that 'poor, decrepid standard' on which was inscribed 'the name of one Boileau'. Yet here, at least, he is nearer to the eighteenth century than to some of his contemporaries: and in his poetry he is sometimes doing completely and with far greater genius what many of the eighteenth-century poets were trying to do.

---

[1] *Jeffrey's Essays from 'The Edinburgh Review'* ('The New Universal Library', n.d.), p. 289.

[2] *The Letters of John Keats*, ed. Maurice Buxton Forman, 1935, p. 108.

V

There is another good reason why originality was lightly stressed in the age of Pope and Johnson. The critics were never tired of repeating that it was the poet's duty to avoid the minute and particular and concentrate on the general. If the poet did so—and most of them did—he was more than ever likely to tread where others had trod before him. So long as the poet wrote or the painter painted 'not for the virtuoso or the natural-ist, but for the common observer of life and nature',[1] there were bound to be resemblances between one work and another. Different poets, as Johnson put it, could hardly avoid hitting on the same ideas when they wrote of Spring or the Sea.

Reflecting on human life, they would, without any communica-tion of opinions, lament the deceitfulness of hope, the fugacity of pleasure, the fragility of beauty, and the frequency of calamity.[2]

Johnson's fullest pronouncement on the necessary predomi-nance of the general over the particular occurs in the tenth chapter of *Rasselas*. The poet, we are told, is to concern himself not with the individual but the species; he is to ignore 'the minuter discriminations, which one may have remarked, and another neglected', and concentrate on those aspects which are so large and general that no one can possibly have missed them. He will do this in his observations on men and women and in his descriptions of nature. It is easy enough to attract readers by appealing to their interest in the local event or the contem-porary topic or the modern fashion, but the poet ought to deal with the eternal and unchanging. 'He must divest himself of the prejudices of his age or country; he must consider right and wrong in their abstracted and invariable state; he must dis-regard present laws and opinions, and rise to general and tran-scendental truths, which will always be the same.' To most modern readers this is, to say the least of it, an austere pro-gramme. Yet it represents Johnson's settled opinion about the business of the poet. 'Great thoughts are always general,' he remarked on another occasion, with a disapproving glance at the Metaphysical poets, 'and consist in positions not limited by exceptions, and in descriptions not descending to minuteness.'[3]

---

[1] Reynolds, *Discourses*, p. 181.    [2] *Rambler*, No. 143, 30 July 1751.
[3] *Lives*, i. 21. See Note C, p. 168.

This view, descending from Aristotle to the neo-classical critics, that the business of the artist is to address himself to the general, not to copy what lies before him but to present an idealized picture of life, is expressed with varying emphasis all through our period. Such is the astonishing variety of nature, Shaftesbury argues, that everything in nature has its own peculiar and original character. If the artist were to try to reproduce just *that*, then everything he expressed would be unlike anything else in the world. Good poets and good painters are well aware of this, and therefore do their best to avoid minuteness and singularity, which would make 'their images or characters appear capricious and fantastical'. It is not that they do not study the individual and the particular; they do, and they must. But from their knowledge of many particulars they form their conception of the ideal.[1]

Among English critics Sir Joshua Reynolds is perhaps the most uncompromising in his demand for idealization in art. Nature, he insists, is not to be too closely copied. The artist who thinks to gain a reputation by minute and faithful copying of what he sees may astonish the gaping ignorant, but he will not impress the judicious. He is to the true painter what the florist or the collector of shells is to the true scientist, a mere accumulator of heterogeneous detail. How different was the practice of Claude Lorraine, who realized that to paint nature as he found it would rarely produce beauty.

His pictures are a composition of the various drafts which he had previously made from various beautiful scenes and prospects.[2]

Similarly the history painter (who corresponds to the epic poet) does not introduce individual portraits into his composition, but paints mankind in general; the portrait painter is necessarily at a disadvantage here, since his sitter is a particular man or woman 'and consequently a defective model'.[3] He can, perhaps, idealize to some extent, but he is handicapped by the necessity of producing an individual and recognizable likeness. But Reynolds goes even farther, and introduces the word 'deformity' to characterize any individual object in nature or any mere representation of that object. When people of vulgar taste see a Dutch painting of a man with a wart on his nose, they ex-

---

[1] *Characteristics*, i. 112 f.          [2] *Discourses*, pp. 37, 54.
[3] Ibid., p. 55.

claim, 'How natural!'; in fact, if they only knew it, nothing could be more unnatural.

Deformity is not nature, but an accidental deviation from her accustomed practice. This general idea therefore ought to be called nature; and nothing else, correctly speaking, has a right to that name.[1]

The wart on a man's nose may seem too extreme an example to allow Reynolds to build an argument upon it. In fact his case does not rest upon *such* oddities and imperfections:

All the objects which are exhibited to our view by nature, upon close examination will be found to have their blemishes and defects. The most beautiful forms have something about them like weakness, minuteness, or imperfection.[2]

The true artist is therefore the man who has learnt, after prolonged contemplation and intimate experience of nature in all her varied forms, to distinguish—and, if necessary, to create— the one perfect from the innumerable expressions of the imperfect. 'He corrects nature by herself, her imperfect state by her more perfect.' Reynolds does not shrink from the full implications of his paradox: in arriving at perfection the artist may be creating something that he has never actually *seen*. 'He learns to design naturally by drawing his figures unlike to any one object.'[2]

In such perfection there must necessarily be a certain remoteness, a quality of abstraction; but Reynolds does not shrink from that either. Indeed, it is the sort of effect he wants.

The whole beauty and grandeur of the art [he maintains] consists, in my opinion, in being able to get above all singular forms, local customs, particularities, and details of every kind.[2]

Enlarging upon this statement in his Fourth Discourse Reynolds explains that it is only the painter in an inferior style who attempts minute discriminations of the drapery; the clothing worn by an artist's figures should not be recognizably woollen, or linen, or silk, or satin, or velvet, but simply drapery. In the same way the dress in a modern portrait should not belong to the period; it should be timeless, 'with a general air of the antique for the sake of dignity, and . . . something of the modern for the sake of likeness'.[3] Does Reynolds overstate the case?

[1] Ibid., p. 107.          [2] Ibid., p. 30.          [3] Ibid., p. 125.

Those folds of generalized drapery and those bleakly anonymous dresses with 'a general air of the antique' are familiar
features of the portraits of Lely, Kneller, and Reynolds himself.
They do, in fact, impart an air of grandeur and dignity to those
portraits at the expense of that liveliness and individualization
which we find in the portraits of, say, George Stubbs. There
comes a point where the generalizing process may be carried
so far that the individual likeness vanishes altogether. Those
who advocate the expression of the general in preference to the
particular sometimes write as if the ideal to be aimed at was
the complete elimination of all particulars whatsoever. It is an
ideal achieved in the diagrams of Euclid, where the squares and
the triangles have a universal application, and no particular
significance at all. But do we welcome such complete generalization in art? And do we really approve of the artist who consciously endeavours to be not of his age but of all time, which is
in fact no time?

The eighteenth-century poet does not usually avoid all particularization, but in his serious poetry he undoubtedly leans
towards the general:

> How deep yon azure dies the sky!
> Where orbs of gold unnumber'd lye,
> While thro' their ranks in silver pride
> The nether crescent seems to glide.
> The slumb'ring breeze forgets to breathe,
> The lake is smooth and clear beneath,
> Where once again the spangled show
> Descends to meet our eyes below.
> The grounds which on the right aspire,
> In dimness from the view retire:
> The left presents a place of graves,
> Whose wall the silent water laves.
> That steeple guides thy doubtful sight
> Among the livid gleams of night.
> There pass with melancholy state,
> By all the solemn heaps of fate,
> And think, as softly-sad you tread
> Above the venerable dead,
> *Time was, like thee they life possest,*
> *And time shall be, that thou shalt rest.*[1]

[1] Chalmers, ix. 364.

Those lines from Parnell's 'Night-Piece on Death' are neither vague nor blurred, but they do leave a *general* impression on the mind. No doubt he had a particular churchyard in mind: not all churchyards are situated by the side of a lake, and not all churches have a steeple. But he avoids detail, and concentrates on 'general properties and large appearances'. It is much the same with Tickell's lines on Addison's funeral:

> Can I forget the dismal night, that gave
> My soul's best part for-ever to the grave!
> How silent did his old companions tread,
> By mid-night lamps, the mansions of the dead,
> Through breathing statues, then unheeded things,
> Through rowes of warriors, and through walks of kings!
> What awe did the slow solemn knell inspire;
> The pealing organ, and the pausing choir;
> The duties by the lawn-robed prelate pay'd,
> And the last words, that dust to dust convey'd.[1]

There is indeed some particularization here, for Tickell is reminding us that Addison was interred in Westminster Abbey; but apart from that he has contented himself with touching upon 'such permanent and striking features as recall the original to every mind'.

Some of the finest writing in eighteenth-century poetry went into the description of character. Here again the poet usually aims at the typical and the general, as in Gay's 'The Birth of the Squire' or in Goldsmith's or Crabbe's sketches of village characters. Goldsmith's schoolmaster in *The Deserted Village* is typical of his kind, and yet he has enough individuality to mark him out from other country pedagogues. Satire invited the eighteenth-century poet to a more individual treatment. In his *Moral Essays* Pope often begins with the individual, though he may end with the type, and in such portraits as that of Orator Henley in the *Dunciad* (iii. 195 ff.) the ridicule falls almost entirely on a particular mountebank. Henley is where he is because he is unlike anyone else. 'None but himself can be his parallel.' Indeed, the twentieth-century reader is apt to find the *Dunciad*, and, to a smaller extent, such poems as *Absalom and Achitophel*, only partially intelligible owing to the fact that the materials out of which they were made are too firmly embedded in the literary or political life of their own day. Poems like

[1] Ibid. xi. 122.

Pope's *Imitations of Horace* or the *Dunciad* perhaps need to be written anew for each generation: the universal element remains, but the particular applications can best be supplied by each generation (and by each nation) out of its own experience. Here, at least, the desire for originality can be reconciled with the equally strong desire for what oft was thought.

Unfriendly critics of the eighteenth century have sometimes suggested that its poets confined themselves to the general (at all events in their descriptions of nature) because they were insensitive to the particular. That seems to be implied in a remark of Joseph Warton:

> If our poets would accustom themselves to contemplate fully every object, before they attempted to describe it, they would not fail of giving their readers more new and more complete images than they generally do.[1]

To Wordsworth it seemed that between the publication of *Paradise Lost* and *The Seasons* there was scarcely 'a single new image of external nature', nor an image already familiar which would indicate that 'the eye of the Poet had been steadily fixed upon his object'.[2] It would not be difficult to disprove this rash statement from the works of Pope alone; but surely Wordsworth is refusing to allow for what is primarily a question, not of observation but of method, of what the poet does with the materials which his observation supplies. The idea that the eighteenth-century poet was less observant than the average Boy Scout of the twentieth century is one that will not bear examination: if he did not fill his poems with sharply individualized descriptions of nature it must have been—it was— because he considered that as a poet something more difficult and more profitable was expected of him. From his own varied experience he distilled those elements which appeared to him to be common to all individual instances. His general, in fact, was the essence of many particulars; he would have considered that mere observation of particular instances was the lowest form of mental life, and he would not have been far wrong. No doubt some second-rate poets and some inferior painters wrote or painted without having familiarized themselves with their object, but that may happen in any age. At all events,

---

[1] *An Essay on the Genius and Writings of Pope*, 1782, i. 47. Vol. i was first published in 1756.

[2] *Wordsworth's Literary Criticism*, p. 185 ('Essay Supplementary to the Preface').

such slovenliness received no support from Johnson or Reynolds.
After urging his students to aim always at general nature, and
to avoid whatever is particular or accidental or local or temporary, Reynolds continues:

I should be sorry, if what is here recommended, should be at all
understood to countenance a careless or indetermined manner of
painting.  For though the painter is to overlook the accidental discriminations of nature, he is to exhibit distinctly, and with precision,
the general forms of things.[1]

And those general forms of things could only be learnt by the
student who had closely observed and carefully reflected upon
many particular examples.

Those who are disposed to disagree with the theory of art so
confidently upheld by Johnson and Reynolds should at least
recognize that this endless search for the universal and unchanging element in human experience involves a noble exercise of the mental faculties.  It calls forth the powers of reflection
in both writer and reader.  'To write on their plan', Johnson
admitted rather grudgingly of the Metaphysical poets, 'it was
at least necessary to read and think.'[2]  The same, *mutatis mutan-
dis*, may be said of Pope and his contemporaries.  Nothing is
easier than to record minute and unrelated particulars—what
I saw, what I heard, what happened to me: a schoolboy will fill
his letter home with such observations.  But the Johnsonian
observation, which after surveying mankind from China to
Peru arrives at a general view of man's nature, is something
far more difficult of attainment.

It is just here that one of those wide shifts of taste has
occurred.  The twentieth-century reader tends to be relatively
uninterested in the general, and sharply aware of and satisfied
with the particular.  Blake's marginal retort to Reynolds, 'To
generalize is to be an idiot.  To particularize is the alone distinction of merit',[3] is much too violent to be characteristic of
the nineteenth century as a whole, and may in any case rest
upon a misinterpretation of Reynolds's meaning.  Yet it is
symptomatic of a change in critical attitude.  In the *Biographia
Literaria*[4] Coleridge asserted that he still believed that poetry
was essentially ideal and should avoid and exclude all accident,

---

[1] *Discourses*, p. 39.                          [2] *Lives*, i. 21.
[3] *The Writings of William Blake*, ed. Geoffrey Keynes, 1925, iii. 13.
[4] Op. cit. ii. 37.

but on an earlier occasion he had remarked that though we may at first be delighted with '*generalities* of nature which can all be expressed in dignified words', later on, as our knowledge of nature becomes more detailed, 'we are delighted with *distinct, vivid ideas*'.[1] From Hazlitt, too, comes a protest that Reynolds's 'vague, vapid, nondescript *ideal* conception, which pretends to unite . . . in reality destroys'. Hazlitt is impressed by the infinite variety in nature: each species and sub-species is capable of its own perfection, and it is the business of the poet or the artist to give to each of them a clear and precise expression.

Sir Joshua's theory limits nature and paralyses art. According to him, the middle form or the average of our various impressions is the source from which all beauty, pleasure, interest, imagination springs. I contend on the contrary that this very variety is good in itself, nor do I agree with him that the whole of nature as it exists in fact is stark naught, and that there is nothing worthy of the contemplation of a wise man but that *ideal perfection* which never existed in the world nor on canvas.[2]

Since Hazlitt's day this awareness of the integrity and significance of the individual has developed to a remarkable extent:

> As kingfishers catch fire, dragonflies draw flame;
> As tumbled over rim in roundy wells
> Stones ring; like each tucked string tells, each hung bell's
> Bow swung finds tongue to fling out broad its name;
> Each mortal thing does one thing and the same:
> Deals out that being indoors each one dwells;
> Selves—goes itself; *myself* it speaks and spells,
> Crying *What I do is me: for that I came.* . . .[3]

Much contemporary art and poetry seems to have severed all connexion with that general truth which was the aim of Johnson and Reynolds, and to base its appeal on its expression not merely of the particular but even of the unique. The painter or sculptor who creates an abstract composition is in the most literal sense creating something that is not in nature—something that God omitted to make. He has moved as far as it is possible to go from what oft was thought; he seeks to avoid recalling any original to the mind, for his composition *is* the

---

[1] *Anima Poetae*, p. 128. See Note D, p. 168.
[2] *Table Talk* ('Bohn' edition), p. 197 f.
[3] *Poems of Gerard Manley Hopkins*, ed. Robert Bridges, 1943, p. 53.

original. So, too, some contemporary poets have given us an imaginative experience that cannot be found elsewhere because it is unique, and is not, and was never meant to be, anything other than a train of individual thought and feeling. 'What I do is me: for that I came.'

The eighteenth-century critic, thinking all the time that the source of pleasure in poetry must be found in some kind of *recognition*,[1] did not sufficiently allow for another sort of pleasure —the enlargement of our experience. To confine the poet to recording what the average reader was likely to have met with in the course of his own experience was, however well meant, an unnecessary restriction. The truth seems to be that there is an experience which we can call imaginative recognition: we can recognize with pleasure what we have never actually met with before. It is in this way that we can take delight in Shelley's two halcyons on the drooping bough—

> two azure halcyons clinging downward
> And thinning one bright bunch of amber berries,
> With quick long beaks . . .[2]

or Wordsworth's description of the daisy (recorded in his seventy-sixth year)—

> The beauty of its star-shaped shadow, thrown
> On the smooth surface of this naked stone[3]—

or Thomas Hardy's entry in his note-book, on 19 January 1920, at the age of seventy-nine:

> Coming back from Talbothays by West Stafford Cross I saw Orion upside down in a pool of water under an oak.[4]

How much eighteenth-century poetry lost from a well-meant endeavour to deal only with 'those characteristicks which are alike obvious to vigilance and carelessness' it would be hard to

---

[1] When the business of the poet is thought to be imitation, it follows that the source of pleasure in poetry must lie in some sort of recognition by the reader, who is reminded of something he has already experienced. 'Poetry being imitation', Steele argues, 'and . . . that imitation being the best which deceives the most easily, it follows that we must take up the customs which are most familiar or universally known, *since no man can be deceived or delighted with the imitation of what he is ignorant of'* (*Guardian*, No. 30, 15 Apr. 1713). Poetry, Johnson writes, cannot 'dissect the latent qualities of things without losing its general power of gratifying every mind *by recalling its own conceptions*' (*Rambler*, No. 36, 21 July 1750).

[2] *Prometheus Unbound*, III. iv. 80 ff.

[3] *Poetical Works*, ed. John Morley, 1888, p. 790.

[4] Florence E. Hardy, *The Later Years of Thomas Hardy*, 1930, p. 201.

say. The habit of seeing things—'the minuter discriminations, which one may have remarked and another neglected'[1]—may possibly have lapsed to some extent: we do not go on observing what we know we cannot use. But the trouble was due rather to the poet's hesitation (the result of current literary theory) to use what he had seen. Towards the end of the century those inhibitions begin to disappear. In the poetry of Cowper, for example, we often meet with entirely fresh and original observation, a seizing upon the thing seen however unusual or infrequent it may be. 'The Winter Morning Walk' opens with a description of how in the slanting rays of the winter sun long shadows are cast upon the snow:

> Mine, spindling into longitude immense,
> In spite of gravity, and sage remark
> That I myself am but a fleeting shade,
> Provokes me to a smile. With eye askance
> I view the muscular proportioned limb
> Transformed to a lean shank. The shapeless pair,
> As they designed to mock me, at my side
> Take step for step; and as I near approach
> The cottage, walk along the plastered wall,
> Preposterous sight! the legs without the man.[2]

This is odd and fantastic, and certainly one of the 'minuter discriminations': if we had met with it much earlier in the century it would almost certainly have been in burlesque or mock-heroic—not in a serious poem, and only there at all for the sake of illustrating some thought.

From Cowper's perhaps unconscious practice it is only a step to Wordsworth's conscious endeavour to record what had hitherto escaped observation, or at least had never been expressed in verse. In a note which he dictated to Miss Fenwick about his early poem, *An Evening Walk*, Wordsworth claimed that there was not a single image that he had not observed for himself, and that though he was now in his seventy-third year he could still remember when and where most of them were first noticed by him. He quotes two lines:

> And, fronting the bright west, yon oak entwines
> Its darkening boughs and leaves, in stronger lines—

---

[1] Johnson, *Rasselas*, ch. x. Cf. p. 23.
[2] *The Task*, v. 11 ff.

and then comments:

This is feebly and imperfectly expressed, but I recollect distinctly the very spot where this first struck me. It was in the way between Hawkshead and Ambleside, and gave me extreme pleasure. The moment was important in my poetical history; for I date from it my consciousness of the infinite variety of natural appearances which had been unnoticed by the poets of any age or country, so far as I was acquainted with them; and I made a resolution to supply, in some degree, the deficiency. I could not have been at that time above 14 years of age.[1]

Wordsworth's resolution has all the marks of the schoolboy's passion for collecting—not stamps, or coins, or beetles in this case, but observations of natural phenomena. So stated, his aim may appear to be worthy enough, but it hardly indicates that at this early stage he had the mind of a poet. Such descriptions as the boy Wordsworth was contemplating have in them a good deal of that matter-of-factness of which many of his critics have complained; they do not become poetry merely because they are descriptions of nature. An eighteenth-century reader might have found a good deal to admire in *An Evening Walk*, but he would almost certainly have asked the poet, 'What use are you making of all this minute description? What general idea, what universal human experience does it serve to illustrate? At present we cannot see the wood for the trees. *Is* there a wood at all?'

[1] *The Poetical Works of William Wordsworth*, ed. E. de Selincourt, 1940, i. 318 f.

# THE BACKGROUND (2)

I

IF the seventeenth century had been an age of religious fervour it had also been a time of political upheaval and experiment. Here again the eighteenth century was all for settling down and strengthening the things that remained after the Revolution settlement of 1689. It is easy to be impatient with such conservatism if we forget the troubled age from which it emerged. Charles II's determination not to go on his travels again was shared, consciously or unconsciously, by most of his subjects, and by their children and grandchildren. In 1715, and again in 1745, the rebels were put down without much difficulty, not because most Englishmen loved the Hanoverians or thought they had the best of all possible governments—no true-born Englishman ever thinks that—but because very few of them were willing to reopen a question that had been settled, and fewer still believed that any change could be worth the cost of another civil war. The bias of the times was therefore towards the established order, and against innovation, experiment, and any questioning of fundamental principles.

The new century's dislike of innovation sometimes comes out in the oddest of ways. When, in 1783, public executions were at last abolished and the old saturnalia at Tyburn came to an end, Dr. Johnson resisted the suggestion that this was an improvement. 'No, Sir, (said he, eagerly) it is *not* an improvement'; and then, after giving several reasons in favour of the old system, he ended, almost plaintively: 'Why is all this to be swept away?'[1] Seven years later, the same English fear of innovation, the dread of letting loose forces which sought to overturn the established order, found powerful expression in Burke's *Reflections on the Revolution in France*:

We are resolved to keep an established church, an established monarchy, an established aristocracy, and an established democracy, each in the degree it exists, and in no greater. . . . It has been the misfortune (not as these gentlemen think it, the glory) of this age, that everything is to be discussed, as if the constitution of our

[1] Boswell, *Life*, iv. 188.

country were to be always a subject rather of altercation than enjoyment.[1]

Why should these things be swept away? Why should they even be discussed? The attitude is the same in both men: let well alone, and even if it is not so well, let it alone just the same, lest worse should follow. We should learn to reverence, and seek to preserve, the wisdom of our ancestors. Unlike those revolutionary Frenchmen,

We are afraid to put men to live and trade each on his own private stock of reason; because we suspect that the stock in each man is small, and that the individuals would do better to avail themselves of the general bank and capital of nations and of ages.[2]

The *status quo* which Burke defends so eloquently had come in, of course, with the Revolution of 1688; but that was all a long, long time ago. What mattered to Burke, and to the great majority of his contemporaries, was that never again should the country have to face fundamental issues about Church and State and the whole structure of society.

It is not surprising that this strong conservative tendency should have spread to literature and the arts. When Sir Joshua Reynolds told his students that 'the old has that great advantage of having custom and prejudice on its side', and warned them against 'the evil and confusion which innovation always brings with it',[3] he was voicing what must have seemed to most of his hearers an obvious truth. To-day such sentiments might still be accepted from a President of the Royal Academy with a sort of amused tolerance, but coming from anyone under fifty they would probably be regarded as a sign of intellectual incompetence. In the age of Johnson and Reynolds and Burke they were the sentiments of most intelligent people. Why not? It is just as intelligent to be prejudiced in favour of the old because it is old, as to be biased in favour of the new because it is new.

What men have grown accustomed to comes, in a stable period, to seem right and inevitable. Not only has it 'the right of possession', but it enjoys the further advantage of having behind it the consensus of opinion. We shall never understand the eighteenth century if we do not recognize its widespread desire for agreement, not only on fundamentals but also on as

---

[1] Op. cit. ('World's Classics' ed.), p. 100.
[2] Ibid., p. 95.                              [3] *Discourses*, pp. 124, 125.

many of the secondary matters as possible. This desire for agreement was sharpened by memories of violent disagreement and disorder in the not remote past, and reinforced in a rational age by the comfortable belief that agreement was attainable among reasonable men. In literature and in art, no less than in politics and religion, it was felt that agreement should and could be reached, and by the middle of the century it was generally thought that it had been reached. With this belief went the further conviction that after a long process of trial and error poetry had at last reached a satisfactory form of expression, and had now little need for further innovations.

We can watch this idea gradually hardening as the decades go by. Already in Dryden we come upon the notion that English poetry did not come to full maturity until Waller and Denham. Waller 'first made writing easily an art', and Denham's *Cooper's Hill* 'ever will be the exact standard of good writing'.[1] The emphasis with Dryden is generally on the vast improvement in the art of poetry since these two poets first showed the way. But even in Dryden we meet with the further idea that English poetry is getting nearer perfection, or, at any rate, that perfection is attainable and will be reached only by proceeding farther along the lines now laid down for the poet. 'If natural causes be more known now than in the time of Aristotle, because more studied, it follows that poesy and other arts may, with the same pains, arrive still nearer to perfection.'[2] The analogy, it will be noticed, is with science; the arts are to advance in the same way as the natural sciences. When we come to Johnson, nearly a hundred years later, we get the impression that Dryden's vision has been fulfilled. After a long period of uncertainty and experiment, poetry had arrived at a satisfactory, and apparently final, mode of expression. The English Muse had grown up; the old inarticulate and un-disciplined days of her childhood were past.

New sentiments and new images others may produce, but to attempt any further improvement of versification will be dangerous. Art and diligence have now done their best, and what shall be added will be the effort of tedious toil and needless curiosity.[3]

This sounds strange to modern ears. It is rather like saying: 'We have now evolved a satisfactory teapot, one that is pleasant

---

[1] *Essays*, i. 7.                                          [2] Ibid. i. 44.
[3] Johnson, *Lives*, iii. 251.

to look at, and that has a practical and sensible spout. New decorative effects others may produce, but to attempt any reformation in the design will be dangerous. We are not likely after all those years to improve on what we have got, and we might easily get something much less satisfactory. So why go on fiddling with teapot design? We have surely reached agreement on what is best.' The modern mind, less hostile to innovation, may be puzzled by Johnson's insistence on stabilizing the form of poetry; but Johnson, standing at the end of a long and orderly evolution, did not consider that any good purpose could be served by tampering now with the form of poetry. Even to-day, when most people think differently about those matters, few would care to see any sweeping alterations in, say, the University Boat Race. The race might be rowed with six men, or in a wider boat, or on a shorter or a longer course; but most rowing men would resent such innovations as 'the effort of tedious toil and needless curiosity'.

Where there was still room in eighteenth-century poetry for individual choice or caprice in points of poetic technique, Johnson was characteristically eager for some general agreement, so that future poets might be under no misapprehension as to what was allowable and what was not.

Considering the metrical art simply as a science [he wrote] and consequently excluding all casualty, we must allow that triplets and alexandrines inserted by caprice are interruptions of that constancy to which science aspires. And though the variety which they produce may very justly be desired, yet to make our poetry exact there ought to be some stated mode of admitting them.[1]

'It is all right so long as we know what you are doing', Johnson is saying to the poet. 'But we must have a ruling on this point; we can't go on leaving the decision to the individual, for then we shall never know where we are. As rational people we ought to be able to reach some agreement about the use of alexandrines and triplets, and when we have come to a decision we ought to stick to it.'

## II

Fear of innovation, hostility to the new and the untried, were the negative aspects of eighteenth-century conservatism; on the positive side we may count the efforts to establish, and

[1] Johnson, *Lives*, i. 468.

afterwards to maintain, a reasonable way of life and a strong and stable culture. A compact and well-ordered society becomes gradually conscious of certain standards which are shared by all men of good sense and good taste, and it is then the business of that society to reinforce and extend them. In a democratic community those standards will be enforced with a minimum of actual compulsion; they will be maintained by the steady pressure of public opinion acting through its statesmen, preachers, professional and business men, writers and artists. In the age of Dryden or Defoe the author found guilty of seditious writing or the printer of seditious publishing might be imprisoned or pilloried; but as society became surer of itself such drastic punishment became less necessary, and the merely odd and eccentric individual was ridiculed into harmlessness or conformity, or dismissed as a madman.

In an unstable and revolutionary age such as the twentieth century, there will be no such community of belief (unless it is enforced with all the prestige and coercive power of State control), but rather a constant clash between the old and the new. There will be much argument but little agreement, much experiment but few standards. So far as the writer is concerned, there will be plenty to write about in a revolutionary period, but unusual difficulty in establishing contact with the reader; the really new writer will have to be content with the encouragement of the discriminating few and their intellectual toadies (the Witwouds, in fact, as well as the Mirabells) until such time as the common reader (Matthew Arnold's 'elephantine main body') catches up with him. In a period of stability, on the other hand, the new writer will be new only as to-morrow morning is new; his experience and his mode of expressing it will be fresh, but they will also be familiar. He will proceed upon the existing assumptions, and so he will have little difficulty in carrying his reader with him.

In the eighteenth century, as we shall see,[1] the standards were formed at the top and flowed downwards to the rank and file; but this is the usual state of affairs in non-revolutionary periods, or what Arnold called 'epochs of concentration'. We can see the process beautifully at work in eighteenth-century architecture. There was, indeed, a certain amount of actual restraint in the form of building laws to maintain a consistent elevation

[1] See p. 60 f.

in a row of urban houses or to prevent outrageous eccentricities
and unsocial outbursts of architectural self-expression. But the
dignity and restraint of Georgian houses and public buildings
were much more the outcome of a fine tradition, of the silent
pressure of good taste, and of standards willingly accepted and
consciously approved. The Burlingtons did not *impose* their
taste on the eighteenth century; they gained their ends by
example and persuasion. When once good taste has established
itself it becomes as hard to displace as the bad taste of less fortunate periods.

None the less the price of order and beauty and dignity is
eternal vigilance; and it was one of the most important func-
tions of the eighteenth-century writers to maintain and cherish
the standards of polite society, not only in matters of taste and
manners, but also in morality and religion. This they did,
partly by a direct expression of approval, as when Pope celebrated the virtues of Ralph Allen or The Man of Ross, but more
characteristically, perhaps, by means of satire. The importance
of satire in eighteenth-century poetry can only be grasped if
we remember that as often as not the satirist was deliberately
reinforcing the agreed standards of the age by pointing at the
eccentric, the anti-social, the freethinker, the profligate, the
antinomian. The greater part of the century's rich and varied
satire (though this generalization will not always hold true for
Swift) was written by men who were fully at one with the
standards of the day and who could count upon the immediate
acquiescence of all but a few of their readers. Without this
common ground between writer and reader, Addison and
Steele, Pope and Fielding, could not have written as they did.
When Byron writes satire at the beginning, or Shaw at the
end, of the nineteenth century, it is of a very different order—
consciously impudent and provocative, because, however sure
either Byron or Shaw may be of *himself*, he knows that he is
flying in the face of public opinion. Most eighteenth-century
satire is therefore addressed to those who are already converted
(as most sermons are preached to those who are already saved);
but by continually keeping the edge of distinction sharp, the
satirists helped to make their readers more continually and
more completely aware of their own half-conscious and un-
spoken beliefs.

That the satire of Pope and his followers also tended to

discourage originality and to maintain the established order of beliefs beyond their usefulness is unfortunately true; the good and the bad fell in swathes before the satirist's onslaught. Anyone who challenged the existing order in religion (Collins, Clarke, Toland, Tindall, Whitefield, Wesley), in morality (Mandeville), in literature (Defoe, Mrs. Centlivre, Colley Cibber), in scholarship (Bentley, Theobald), in architecture (Vanbrugh), was liable to ridicule and the calculated distortion of the satirist. If some satirists are like vagrant message-boys who chalk rude remarks on the front door and run away, Pope and his friends were much more in the position of the householder who finds his own or his neighbour's doors scribbled upon and proceeds to rub out the marks, and, if possible, expose the culprit. The eighteenth-century satirist was the child of a stable society, and he repaid the advantages of being born into a settled age by constantly reinforcing its sturdy foundations. That, at any rate, holds true for the first half of the century. But since satire is a weapon that can be drawn in any cause, we find it sometimes towards the end of our period being turned against the established order, or, as in Crabbe's *Village*, against some worn-out literary convention. By that time, however, the old order was itself crumbling, and Crabbe could count on plenty of readers who would agree with him.

If Pope occasionally ridicules the diversions of the polite society that formed the main body of his readers, that only tells us that polite society in the eighteenth century, as in other periods, ran occasionally into excesses. The standards which Pope strove to maintain were not just the trivial conventions or prejudices of the fashionable and the well-to-do. So far as they can be defined at all they were the standards of the man of sense, alive to every manifestation of folly and extravagance, every departure from right reason and moderation and good taste. The vanities of polite society are ridiculed in *The Rape of the Lock*; tasteless extravagance and luxury in *Moral Essays*, III and IV; hack-writers, the contemporary theatre, schools and universities, the follies of empty-headed peers, and much else in *The Dunciad* and the *Imitations of Horace*.

Among all the standards that had to be kept up were those of good literature. Here again we must remember the situation confronting English writers after the Restoration if we are to understand the bias of their literary criticism and their outlook on the writers of the previous age. Rightly or wrongly, Dryden believed that poetry in his own day was sharing in a general rise in the level of civilization. The improvements which he believed he saw in contemporary poetry were comparable to such improvements as piped water and modern windows and fire-places in houses; Englishmen were learning—in London at any rate—to live in a more civilized way, and now they were learning to write with the same up-to-date finish and distinction as the French. The dramatic writers of what Dryden always calls 'the last age'—Shakespeare, Jonson, and Fletcher—were men of great natural genius, but he felt that they had lived and written in rude and unpolished times, and that their work was everywhere deficient in that sort of culture which a polite society alone can give to a writer. They were altogether too violent, too metaphorical, too eager, too emphatic; their wit was coarse or childish or pedantic, and they wrote in general by the mere light of nature. Only a narrow isthmus of years separated the age of Etherege and Dryden from that of the Puritan bigots with their unmannerly excess of zeal and their uncouth language; indeed, these same Puritans were still at large in the City, and it was only at Court that the new, urbane, well-ordered way of living and writing was consistently possible. The new standards were therefore far from secure yet, and it was the self-imposed task of men like Etherege in his comedies, or young noblemen of taste like Lord Mulgrave or Lord Roscommon in their poems, to reinforce them by example and precept.

Quite apart from the danger that literature might relapse into the old formlessness and boisterousness (Shadwell, for instance, has much of the crude, hearty, open-air vigour of the Elizabethans), there was a new danger arising from the very advances that were being made. The more settled times of Charles II had hatched out swarms of new writers, imperfectly educated and not noticeably endowed with wit—'the mob of gentlemen who wrote with ease', the aristocratic and middle-class amateurs who could turn out 'a copy of verses'. 'Never was there known so many versifyers', says one observer in the year 1685, 'and so few poets; every ass that's romantick believes he's inspir'd, and none have been so forward to teach others as those who cannot write themselves. . . . Every fop that falls in love thinks he has a right to make songs, and all kind of people that are gifted with the least knowledge of Latin and Greek pretend to translate.'[1] This rabble of new writers had to be educated in the new literary standards (of which they were largely ignorant) if the good work was not to be all undone. Addressing Thomas Creech, the translator of Lucretius, in 1683, Otway complains of the 'lousy madrigalls' and the 'nasty farce' which pass for lyric poetry and comedy.

> No, since we live in such a fulsome age,
> When nonsense loads the press, and choaks the stage,
> When block-heads will claym wit in nature's spight,
> And every dunce that starves presumes to write,
> Exert your self, defend the Muse's cause . . . .
> For of all nature's works we most should scorn
> The thing who thinks himself a poet born.
> Unbred, untaught he rhymes, yet hardly spells,
> And senslessly, as squirrels jangle bells.
> Such things, sir, here abound . . . .[2]

Some fifty years later the *Dunciad* was directed against a new generation of those literary upstarts (now vastly increased in numbers owing to the rapid development of literary journalism and the growth of the reading public), and whatever private scores he may be settling, Pope is genuinely concerned to maintain the threatened standards of polite literature. The constant insistence on the Rules must therefore be related in the early part of our period to a determination to consolidate gains recently made, to keep under cultivation territory reclaimed from the swamp, and later, in the age of Johnson, to a more purely conservative tendency to keep inviolate what had proved so successful in the experience of several literary generations.

In a period when fundamental questions of principle have been largely settled—or when, at any rate, they are not raised in an acute form—secondary matters, such as how to write poetry, become topics of major importance. During the Civil War Englishmen had been too violently engaged in political and religious strife to have either the time or the inclination to dispute about such trifles as the Unities or the introduction of Christian machinery into epic poetry. But men must have some outlet for their enthusiasm and their natural irritability, and in

[1] Robert Wolseley, Preface to *Valentinian*, Spingarn, iii. 12 f.
[2] *The Works of Thomas Otway*, ed. J. C. Ghosh, 1932, ii. 439 f. (Chalmers, viii. 296).

the cooler temperature of Charles II's reign (and still more in the age of Anne and the first Georges) literary questions seemed well worth arguing about. Whatever we may think of the writers themselves, the prestige of literature never stood higher than it did in the days of Pope and Johnson. As early as 1682 the Earl of Mulgrave could write:

> Of things in which mankind does most excell,
> Nature's chief master-piece is writing well,[1]

and the young Pope liked the second line well enough to incorporate it in his *Essay on Criticism*. But in what other age would such a statement have proved so acceptable? Not, certainly, in the age of Milton, and not by many men in the age of Wordsworth and Shelley. No doubt poetry was often, in a century of polite conversation, just another thing to talk about; there were too many Dick Minims in society, too many of those self-satisfied talkers who, as Steele puts it, 'imagine that their making shrewd observations upon the polite arts gives them a pretty figure'.[2] But the evidence is overwhelming that a very large number of people in the eighteenth century really cared about poetry, though it was mainly classical or their own neo-classical poetry that they were able to enjoy. To Pope and Johnson, and to lesser men like John Dennis, good literature, the separating of the good from the bad, and the maintaining of a sound literary tradition, were matters of the first importance. Though Johnson was aware that Pope's immediate motive for writing the *Dunciad* was the desire for revenge, he was also alive to its broader implications:

> If bad writers were to pass without reprehension what should restrain them? . . . All truth is valuable, and satirical criticism may be considered as useful when it rectifies error and improves judgement: he that refines the publick taste is a publick benefactor.[3]

---

[1] *An Essay on Poetry*, ll. 1–2 (Chalmers, x. 91).
[2] *Guardian*, No. 12, 25 Mar. 1713.
[3] Johnson, *Lives*, iii. 241 f.

# III
# READERS AND WRITERS

## I

WHATEVER may be true of other periods, the poets of the eighteenth century wrote their poetry fully intending that it should be read. It is therefore of some importance to know the sort of public they had in mind. If we know what people made a habit of reading the new poems as they came out we shall be in a better position to understand why the poets wrote as they did; for though they did not write *at* their public they did unquestionably write for a public whose tastes they knew, and probably shared, and whose views on poetry they would not normally wish to flout.

Who, then, read Pope and Gay and Johnson? Who read Tickell and Paul Whitehead and James Bramston, the Armstrongs and Somervilles, the Mallets and Mickles, and scores of other half-forgotten poets? We know that Lord Chesterfield and Lady Mary Wortley Montagu read and enjoyed the poetry of their contemporaries, but we also happen to know that Stephen Duck, the Wiltshire thresher, read *Paradise Lost* and Pope's *Messiah*, and that he had a friend who had been a footman for some years in London and who had there bought a number of books which they afterwards read together.[1] Between those two extremes lies the greater part of the population of England, which in the first half of the eighteenth century amounted to about six millions. We may, however, reach some more definite conclusions if we can answer another question: Who *bought* eighteenth-century poetry? How many people in 1700 or 1750 could afford to buy modern poetry as it came from the press? For the contemporaries of Addison and Pope there were almost no circulating libraries available, and though a number of the new poems might be found lying about on coffee-house tables along with the newspapers and other periodicals, it is safe to say that the reader of poetry had either to buy a copy for himself or else borrow one from a friend.

We can form a rough estimate of those who could afford to buy the new poems as they came out if we set the price of books

---

[1] Joseph Spence, *A Full and Authentick Account of Stephen Duck* . . ., 1731, p. 7 f.

opposite the average income of the period. There will always be Stephen Ducks who will go without food to purchase a book, but they may be safely left out of the calculation. On such evidence as is available it becomes clear that to most Englishmen in the eighteenth century poetry was economically a luxury, and that the public which habitually bought new books must have been confined to a relatively small class. For the lower ranges of income statistics are plentiful. We need go no lower in the scale than artisans and handicraftsmen, since with them we touch the fringe of illiteracy; their annual income averaged about £40 throughout the century. The average for the shopkeeper and tradesman class was only a little more, though obviously the upper limit might be a good deal higher. For this large lower-middle class an income of £50 a year was above rather than below the average. The cost of living was a good deal lower than it is to-day, but clothing was not particularly cheap, and among the upper classes with their perukes, silk stockings, linen shirts, lace ruffles, and silver-buckled shoes (to confine the estimate to one sex) it was relatively dearer than it is to-day. Rents were lower, and servants' wages much lower; but then more servants were kept, and they had to be fed and to some extent clothed by their employers. The wonder is that lower-middle-class people lived as well as they did; but obviously they had little left over to spend on the last new poem or play, even if they had wanted to read it.

The book-buying public was therefore to be found mainly among the upper classes. Here, unfortunately, statistics of average income are far less plentiful, and much more subject to variation within the class. A contemporary estimate[1] still respected by economic historians (for want, perhaps, of anything better) puts the average income of temporal lords at £2,800; of baronets at £880; of esquires at £450; and of other gentlemen at £280. To this we might add that the Law was a profitable vocation, and that many of the gentlemen able to form extensive libraries were in fact lawyers. On the other hand, the great majority of the minor clergy were little better off than tradesmen, though their position was considerably better by 1800 than it had been in 1700. The esquire with £450 might easily

---

[1] By Gregory King, in his *Natural and Political Observations* (1696), published in George Chalmers, *Estimate of the Comparative Strength of Great Britain*, 1801, and frequently cited by historians.

find that his various expenses left little over for the buying of books. When he came to Town with his family in the winter they expected him to find money for fashionable lodgings, for visits to the theatre, to the opera (where a seat, as the Branghtons in *Evelina* were to discover, might cost him a guinea), to concerts of vocal and instrumental music (tickets from five shillings to a guinea), to balls and ridottos, Ranelagh and other fashionable places of resort; and he himself would probably wish to dine with his friends at expensive eating-houses like Locket's or the Blue Posts. Even if he were unencumbered with a wife and family and preferred to spend his money in buying books rather than in running after the pleasures of the Town, poetry was only one of several sorts of literature he might wish to buy. Poetry competed in the literary market with political pamphlets, plays, travel books, history, sermons, technical and professional books (often expensive), the *Tatler*, the *Spectator*, and their successors, and, as the century advanced, with more and more prose fiction.

As for the cost of books in this age of low incomes, it was comparatively high. The average price of a new play, published in quarto and sold 'stitched', was eighteen pence; cheaper editions in duodecimo might follow. New poems of the length of Pope's *Epistle to Dr. Arbuthnot* (419 lines) were usually first published in folio or quarto and sold at eighteen pence. *The Dunciad Variorum* (1729) cost 6s. 6d., and *The Dunciad in Four Books* (1743), 7s. 6d.; but these were both large quarto volumes, swollen by Pope's prose commentary and intended, as part of the joke, to present a pompous appearance. Poetical miscellanies running to 250–300 pages in octavo usually cost five or six shillings. Such prices were prohibitive for a large section of the community, and must have acted as a serious deterrent to many gentlemen of middling means. In the circumstances the sale of poetry throughout the century is remarkable.

That there was a public willing to buy poetry and yet discouraged by the bookseller's prices may be seen from the many pirated editions of poems sold at cut prices. In the first decade of the century Henry Hills made a practice of pirating poems and printing them on cheap paper. Defoe's *Jure Divino*, published in folio and sold to subscribers at ten shillings, was promptly pirated in an octavo edition that sold at five shillings, and this edition was undercut not long afterwards by another in chapbook form selling at sixpence. In 1729 a number of booksellers pirated the *Dunciad*, and issued an advertisement claiming that the public had been 'insulted' by having to pay 6*s*. 6*d*. for 'the pompous Quarto Edition' when they could now have the same book for two shillings. Examples of such piracies could be multiplied.

In the later decades of the century cheap editions of the English classics became more numerous. The works of poets and prose writers were often issued serially, and the parts later bound together as a book. By 1782 the German traveller Moritz was able to remark on the familiarity of the English people with the great writers of their own country.

The English national authors are in all hands, and read by all people, of which the innumerable editions they have gone through are a sufficient proof. My landlady, who is only a tailor's widow, reads her Milton; and tells me that her late husband first fell in love with her on this very account, because she read Milton with such proper emphasis.[1]

He goes on to note how

the quick sale of the classical authors is here promoted also by cheap and convenient editions. They have them all bound in pocket volumes, as well as in a more pompous style[2]—

and how, too, it is possible to pick up good books for a penny or a halfpenny on the stalls of second-hand dealers.

From this and other sources we know that the reading public was steadily increasing as the century advanced. But those new readers at the lower income-levels had little effect on the course of contemporary literature. What they had read had rarely been written for *them*; they were merely reading in a cheaper format what had already been published, and they had to take what the publisher in his wisdom thought fit to reprint for them. Occasionally an eighteenth-century poet deliberately sought the widest possible public. Sir Richard Blackmore claimed that he had adapted his *Creation* to 'the general apprehension and capacity of mankind', by trying to write as clearly as possible, by using 'easy and familiar expression', and by avoiding 'any term of art, or any phrase peculiar to the writing and conversation of learned men'.[3] Defoe's *True-Born Englishman* and his *Jure*

---

[1] C. P. Moritz, *Travels in England in 1782* (1886 ed.), p. 35.
[2] Ibid.                                                    [3] The Preface.

*Divino*, Isaac Watts's *Divine Songs attempted in Easy Language for the Use of Children*, the hymns of the Methodists, were all addressed to the unlearned, though their value is more often hortatory or educational than literary. But then there is Swift. It was his practice, we are told, to have two of his men-servants brought in to listen to his poems being read, 'which, if they did not comprehend, he would alter and amend, until they understood it perfectly well, and then would say, *This will do; for I write to the vulgar, more than to the learned.*'[1] How well he succeeded may be seen on almost any page of his poetical works, where the idiomatic and familiar style carries his meaning easily and forcibly to the least learned reader. But here, as in some other matters, Swift was not wholly at one with his age. This conscious ignoring of the polite was part of 'Dr. Swift's odd way', and aroused no protest because everyone knew that Swift was himself one of the polite, a learned man, and one used to courts and the conversation of gentlemen. Swift was a law to himself; he did not absolve other writers from their obligations to polite society. The eighteenth-century poet who wished his poems to make their way with the reading public, and the pub-lisher who hoped to live by selling them, still counted—in the first instance, at least—on the patronage of the upper classes of society; and those polite readers had a clear, and in some re-spects limited, conception of what poetry was and how it should be written.

By the first decades of the nineteenth century a change was clearly on the way. The fact that John Murray could pay Crabbe £3,000 for his *Tales of the Hall* (1819), and that two years earlier Byron asked £2,500 for the fourth canto of *Childe Harold* and got £2,000, points unmistakably to a very con-siderable extension of the public for poetry, and also (it may be added) to a rise in the national income. In 1764 Goldsmith had received twenty guineas for *The Traveller*; Johnson had ten guineas for *London* (1738), and fifteen for *The Vanity of Human Wishes* (1749). Francis Jeffrey, who as editor of the *Edinburgh Review* was in a position to make a good guess, estimated in 1812 that there were probably 'not less than 200,000 persons who read for amusement or instruction, among the middling classes of society'. By the 'middling classes' he meant 'almost

---

[1] *Works*, 1762, vol. i, 'To the Reader'; cited by Harold Williams, *The Poems of Jonathan Swift*, 1937, i, p. xxxiv.

all those who are below the sphere of what is called fashionable or public life'. In the higher ranks of society he reckoned 'not as many as 20,000'.[1] He would certainly have arrived at a lower estimate in 1712—the year, incidentally, in which *The Rape of the Lock* first appeared in print. As late as 1753 the poet Armstrong was not prepared to put the fashionable class (in London alone) at much more than 12,000:

> Range from Tower-hill all London to the Fleet,
> Thence round the Temple t'utmost Grosvenor-street:
> Take in your route both Gray's and Lincoln's Inn;
> Miss not, be sure, my lords and gentlemen;
> You'll hardly raise, as I with Petty guess,
> Above twelve thousand men of taste; unless
> In desperate times a connoisseur may pass.[2]

It was those men and women of taste, whatever precisely their numbers may have been, who were the main supporters of Pope's poetry during his lifetime. It was for them that Nicholas Rowe wrote tragedies and Handel operas, and for them that Thomas Chippendale, a little later, designed furniture, Sir Joshua Reynolds painted portraits, and the Adam brothers built town and country houses. By the middle of the nineteenth century this aristocracy is no longer imposing its tastes so exclusively on the various arts; it is being displaced by a new moneyed class, and by a new middle class with less cultivated tastes and cruder responses.

It is not generally thought that this new middle class did much good to architecture (to take what is perhaps the most striking example) or indeed to any of the fine or the applied arts, but there is a widespread impression that the change which came over society in the nineteenth century brought with it nothing but good to poetry. It may be so; but if it is so, it requires more explanation than it appears ever to have been given. Why should the aristocratic taste that produced Bedford Square be so widely approved, and the aristocratic taste that produced Pope's *Eloisa to Abelard* be so often ridiculed and condemned? Have we one set of values for architecture and quite a different set for poetry? Or does the aristocratic taste express itself more satisfactorily in architecture than in poetry? For the present it is enough to note that the charge brought against

---

[1] *Jeffrey's Essays from 'The Edinburgh Review'*, ed. cit., p. 337.
[2] Chalmers, xvi. 538.

eighteenth-century poetry by Wordsworth—that it is addressed
to a particular class of society, and not to mankind in general—
is on the whole justified. It distressed Wordsworth to find

> How we mislead each other; above all
> How books mislead us, seeking their reward
> From judgments of the wealthy few, who see
> By artificial lights; how they debase
> The many for the pleasure of the few—

how, too, they continually reflect the prejudices of this 'wealthy
few' by emphasizing

> Extrinsic differences, the outward marks
> Whereby society has parted man
> From man—

and how, in so doing, they 'neglect the universal heart'.[1] This
heavy charge cannot be lightly dismissed. For good or for ill
(and Wordsworth had no doubt which it was) eighteenth-
century poetry is fundamentally aristocratic. The poet of the
period is not so much 'a man speaking to men' as a man speaking to men like himself, or to one rather higher in the social
scale. His standards, his values, his emotions and intellectual
interests, his mode of expressing himself, are often characteristic
of the upper class. To that class, or the upper-middle class,
he almost certainly belonged himself, by birth, or education,
or both.

## II

To get some idea of the education of the average poet of this
period we may conveniently turn to those whose lives were
written by Johnson. John Dryden (Westminster and Trinity
College, Cambridge) died in 1700, and may therefore be
omitted from our calculations. Of the forty-three poets in
Johnson's collection whose lives fell either wholly or partially
within the eighteenth century, sixteen were educated at Oxford,
eleven at Cambridge, three at Trinity College, Dublin, and
three at Edinburgh University. Of the remaining ten, three
(Rowe, Dyer, Hammond) were Westminster boys. Two (John
Hughes and Isaac Watts) were Dissenters, and one (Pope) a
Roman Catholic: these were debarred by statute from matricu-
lation at Oxford and Cambridge. Two (Dorset and Sheffield)

---

[1] *Prelude*, xiii. 207 ff.

were noblemen, and, as often happened with the sons of noblemen, were privately educated. This leaves us with only John Gay and Richard Savage, and Gay certainly got a good grounding in classics at his school in Barnstaple. If any of those forty-three poets can be spoken of as uneducated, it is Savage, and even he attended for some years 'a small grammar-school near St. Albans'.[1] No fewer than ten of our poets were Westminster boys, five were at Winchester, four at Eton. Of their parents a considerable number were either noblemen or landed gentlemen, but rather more of them were professional men—lawyers, doctors, or clergymen. Eight of the poets (or about one in five) were the sons of parsons, and no less than thirteen of them (almost one in three) became parsons themselves.

In the eighteenth-century grammar-school the greater part of the young scholar's time was given to the study of Latin and Greek. Day after day, and week after week, he was

Lashed into Latin by the tingling rod.[2]

The contemporary curriculum was set forth, unsympathetically enough, by Thomas Sheridan in his *British Education: Or, The Source of the Disorders of Great Britain* (1756). Sheridan had his own axe to grind, but on the whole his picture is an accurate one.

When a boy can read English with tolerable fluency, which is generally about the age of seven or eight years, he is put to school to learn Latin and Greek; where seven years are employed in acquiring but a moderate skill in those languages. At the age of fifteen or thereabouts, he is removed to one of the universities, where he passes four years more in procuring a more competent knowledge of Greek and Latin, in learning the rudiments of logick, natural philosophy, astronomy, metaphysicks, and the heathen morality. At the age of nineteen or twenty a degree in the arts is taken, and here ends the education of a gentleman.

And what good comes of it? Sheridan asks:

Of the few who, from a love of the arts in which they have been trained, would still keep them alive in their memories, and display their talents to the world, much the greater part serve only to increase the number of bad versifiers, miserable essay writers, and minute philosophers.[3]

---

[1] Johnson, *Lives*, iii. 325.
[2] Gay, 'The Birth of the Squire' l. 46.
[3] Op. cit., p. 17.

It was all expressed more brilliantly in the *Dunciad*, where Pope brings on the ghost of Dr. Busby, the famous headmaster of Westminster School, to boast of his educational régime:

> We ply the memory, we load the brain,
> Bind rebel wit, and double chain on chain,
> Confine the thought, to exercise the breath;
> And keep them in the pale of words till death.[1]

To the last line Pope appends a note: 'By obliging them to get the classic poets by heart, which furnishes them with endless matter for conversation, and verbal amusement for their whole lives.'

But Pope knew better than that. A classical education will produce pedants and bores if it works upon the insensitive and the superficial; but when a Gray or a Matthew Arnold comes in contact with classical literature it will permeate his intellectual and moral being. Something of this sort undoubtedly happened to Addison:

> He employed his first years in the study of the old Greek and Roman writers; whose language and manner he caught at that time of life, as strongly as other young people gain a French accent or a genteel air. An early acquaintance with the classics is what may be called the good-breeding of poetry, as it gives a certain gracefulness which never forsakes a mind that contracted it in youth, but is seldom or never hit by those who would learn it too late.[2]

Addison was perhaps more thoroughly influenced by his classical studies than most men of his time; but if he was steeped in the literature of the ancient world, most of his literary contemporaries were at least strongly tinctured by it. Accustomed at school and college to get the Latin poets by heart, they could scarcely write English poetry without echoing, consciously or unconsciously, their Virgil and Horace, alluding to classical mythology, and employing classical idioms and turns of phrase. So completely was contemporary poetry in the hands of this educated class that when an outsider like Stephen Duck attempted to write poetry he set himself to learn the poetic idiom at second hand. He 'got English', we are told, 'just as *we* get Latin. . . . He study'd *Paradise Lost*, as we study the classics.'[3] So equipped, Duck was able to refer to the harvest

[1] iv. 157 ff.
[2] Thomas Tickell's Preface to his edition of Addison's *Works*, 1721.
[3] Joseph Spence, *A Full and Authentick Account of Stephen Duck*, 1731, pp. 10–11.

as 'Ceres' gifts', and to say of the threshing with which his own arms had so often ached:

> Nor with more heavy strokes could Ætna groan,
> When Vulcan forg'd the arms for Thetis' son.[1]

Fifty years later, a greater than Duck resisted more stubbornly the contemporary idiom; but even Burns was sometimes prompted to show his paces as an orthodox English poet, almost always with unhappy consequences. Had he listened to the well-meant advice of Dr. John Moore, an Anglo-Scot who had made good in London both as a writer and a physician, his excursions into standard English poetry would have been more frequent and more thorough. After advising Burns to 'deal more sparingly, for the future, in the provincial dialect', since that was bound to limit the number of his admirers, Moore goes on to suggest a course of reading. Burns should study

most of the best English poets, and read a little more of history. The Greek and Roman stories you can read in some abridgement, and soon become master of the most brilliant facts, which must highly delight a poetical mind. You *should* also, and very soon *may*, become master of the heathen mythology, to which there are everlasting allusions in all the poets, and which in itself is charmingly fanciful.[2]

'You want to write poetry', Moore is saying to the young provincial. 'Well, this is what poetry is made of nowadays. This is what they want in London; and if you are going to become known outside Ayrshire you will have to remember that we are living in the eighteenth century now, and that polite readers have grown accustomed to a special kind of refined enjoyment when they read poetry. As a small farmer and a young man with only an elementary education, you start with grave disadvantages; but there are certain short cuts to knowledge, and with proper application to books you will soon equip yourself to write poetry that conforms to the recognized standards of the age.' Moore's letter to Burns might almost be called an early example of market research: this and this, he says, is what people are buying and reading to-day; these are the poetical wares that are most in demand in the literary market.

How accurate Dr. Moore was in his diagnosis of contemporary taste may be seen by anyone who takes the trouble to

---

[1] *Poems on Several Subjects*, 1730, p. 16 ('The Thresher's Labour').
[2] 23 May 1787; cited by Hans Hecht, *Robert Burns*, 1936, p. 123 f.

read through one of the most popular miscellanies of the century, Dodsley's *Collection of Poems by Several Hands*, first published in 1748 and reprinted frequently in the next thirty years. We are safe in taking the reader of this miscellany as the typical poetry-reader of the period. Not everything that he liked would be in Dodsley, but there was little in Dodsley that he would not enjoy. Dodsley's poets were men of culture writing for a reader who had enjoyed the same sort of education as their own, and who could therefore share their literary tastes and draw upon the same stock of knowledge. They assumed, for instance (as Dr. Moore assumed), that their readers would be tolerably familiar with at least the less recondite facts of ancient mythology. How far they were prepared to trust to his having this sort of knowledge may be judged from a passage in one of Burke's most popular pamphlets.[1] Driving home one of his favourite points, that the State is an organism of slow growth, and that consequently we should be chary of any sudden innovation, he goes on to say:

By this wise prejudice we are taught to look with horror on those children of their country, who are prompt rashly to hack that aged parent in pieces, and put him into the kettle of magicians, in hopes that by their poisonous weeds, and wild incantations, they may regenerate the paternal constitution, and renovate their father's life.

No doubt there were some of Burke's readers for whom this reference to Medea and the daughters of Pelias meant nothing at all, but many—perhaps the majority—must have been better informed; Burke would hardly have risked clouding his argument with an allusion that was not likely to be fairly generally intelligible. The episode referred to is to be found in Ovid's *Metamorphoses*, Book VII, a work of which any boy who had been educated at an eighteenth-century grammar-school could hardly have been ignorant, and which indeed he probably knew well. This, then, was the sort of knowledge that an eighteenth-century poet or prose-writer counted upon your having. A twentieth-century writer, even if he had such knowledge at his finger-tips, would probably hesitate to make use of it, for he would be much less certain to make himself understood. A shift in the emphasis of education has left the modern reader only moderately equipped to respond to many of those literary

[1] *Reflections on the Revolution in France*, 1790 ('World's Classics' ed., p. 105). I borrow this example from my lecture, *English in the Universities*, 1945.

associations—classical and Biblical, especially—to which neo-classical poetry confidently appeals, and on which in fact it relies for a good deal of its effect. The entire attitude to literary quotation has altered in the twentieth century; it is rare nowadays for an English author to be as allusive as Hazlitt, or (to take an example from more modern times) as the late Professor Saintsbury: Such a change is highly significant, and points to an unlettered reading public. We can hardly suppose that the best contemporary writers are less well read than those of earlier periods; but to be allusive where only a few are likely to understand is bad manners, the mark of the literary snob. To quote Latin to-day in the House of Commons without self-consciousness is almost impossible; in Burke's day such quotation was a commonplace. When Wilkes argued that quotation was a sign of pedantry, Johnson resisted the suggestion: 'No, Sir, it is a good thing; there is a community of mind in it. Classical quotation is the *parole* of literary men all over the world.'[1] Of literary men, it will be noticed; not specifically of the learned. It is just this 'community of mind' which is absent from the far larger and less select reading public of the twentieth century; and the knowledge that was once freely employed to diversify and deepen the significance of literature is rapidly being banished to the cross-word puzzle and the quiz. Such a change may leave the poetry of Wordsworth almost undamaged, but it is bound to impoverish the effect of the far more allusive literature of the eighteenth century.

Yet all the evidence from the eighteenth century does not point in the same direction. How, for instance, are we to interpret the fact that almost every classical poet of note was translated into English verse (some of them several times) during the century? We may readily suppose that a gentleman would often turn an ode of Horace into English verse, and that the more cultured among his friends would be able to appreciate the delicate modern application he had given to the original. But for what readers did Pope translate Homer? The frequent reprinting of this great work in the eighteenth century points rather to a public that could not read Homer in the original than to one which read the translation for the pleasure of comparing the English version with the Greek. The study of Greek, it is true, was less general than the study of Latin. But the

[1] Boswell, *Life*, iv. 102.

frequent translation of the *Aeneid*—by Dryden, Nicholas Brady, Trapp, Pitt, and some half-dozen others—suggests again a public that could enjoy the poem only in English. At the same time, the remarkable popularity of Dryden's *Virgil* and Pope's *Homer*, and the fact that publishers found it worth their while to put out other translations both in verse and in prose, would suggest that Homer and Virgil in English were among the favourite authors of the eighteenth century. There is no comparable demand for them to-day. We must not, of course, make a hard-and-fast division between those who could enjoy Virgil in the original and those who had no Latin at all; many of the readers of Dryden's *Virgil* were probably somewhere between those two extremes. Again, the publication in 1712 of *Mottoes in Five Volumes of the Tatler and to the Two Volumes of the Spectators, Latin and English* indicates, perhaps, an attempt on the part of a publisher to profit from the exasperation of the uninitiated. It was followed by a similar publication in 1737, which included the mottoes to the *Guardian* and the *Freeholder*.

Not to know Latin at all was undoubtedly a handicap to the reader of eighteenth-century poetry. That this was recognized at the time is borne out by an advertisement inserted in the *Craftsman* of 19 April 1729, announcing a new (and comparatively painless) method of learning Latin. The course was intended

as a means of gentlemen's being qualified to receive the truest and utmost diversion and entertainment that can arise from those books that are in polite learning, as essays, plays, poetry etc. by judiciously discerning the fine thoughts, arguments, images, figurative expressions, and elegancies, many of which are taken from the classical writers.

In short, a course in Latin to enable a reader to understand and enjoy English poetry, since so much of the enjoyment must lie in a reader's ability to recognize immediately the conscious echo of Virgil or Horace or Ovid. No one in the eighteenth century doubted that this was one of the *legitimate* pleasures of poetry. Indeed, it extended, as the *Craftsman* advertisement indicates, to all polite literature. In the Preface to *Joseph Andrews* Fielding remarks of the burlesque passages that

many instances will occur in this work, as in the description of battles, and some other places, not necessary to be pointed out to the classical reader; for whose entertainment those parodies or burlesque imitations are chiefly calculated.

It may be that eighteenth-century writers relied overmuch on literary allusion. Johnson has an interesting passage on Gilbert West's imitations of Spenser. They are highly successful performances of their kind; but—

such compositions are not to be reckoned among the great achievements of intellect, because their effect is local and temporary; they appeal not to reason or passion, but to memory, and presuppose an accidental or artificial state of mind. An Imitation of Spenser is nothing to a reader, however acute, by whom Spenser has never been perused. . . . The noblest beauties of art are those of which the effect is co-extended with rational nature, or at least with the whole circle of polished life; what is less than this can be only pretty, the plaything of fashion and the amusement of a day.[1]

Johnson was more conscious than most contemporary critics of the 'common reader', and he realized better than most that much eighteenth-century poetry passed slightly above the common reader's head. But if imitations of Spenser fail to meet the supreme test of great literature, are imitations of Horace—or Juvenal—any better? Johnson might have replied that Horace and Juvenal are comprehended in 'the whole circle of polished life', but in fact he did not choose to make that claim. In discussing Pope's imitations of Horace (the 'relaxations of his genius') he still insisted on the limitations of this kind of literature:

The man of learning may be sometimes surprised and delighted by an unexpected parallel; but the comparison requires knowledge of the original . . . .[2]

And that knowledge, Johnson implies, cannot be fairly *asked* of the reader. (If he already has it, of course, so much the better for him; but the enjoyment of English literature should not depend on one's ability to read a Latin author in the original.) The imitation of classical authors, however, though common enough in eighteenth-century poetry, is an extreme case of that literary inspiration which was so widespread in the period. That modern English poetry could fairly draw some of its nourishment from classical literature Johnson would never have doubted.

[1] *Lives*, iii. 332 f.                    [2] Ibid. iii. 247.

III

If a knowledge of classical literature and mythology was the most important element in the eighteenth-century reader's intellectual equipment, it was far from being the only knowledge required of him or of the poet. Dryden makes several significant pronouncements about the sort of education which he considered essential for the good poet.

A man should be learned in several sciences, and should have a reasonable, philosophical, and in some measure a mathematical head, to be a complete and excellent poet; and besides this, should have experience in all sorts of humours and manners of men; should be thoroughly skilled in conversation, and should have a great knowledge of mankind in general.[1]

In the *Essay of Dramatic Poesy* Neander [Dryden] argues that one 'would be loth to say that he who is endued with a sound judgment has no need of history, geography, or moral philosophy to write correctly'.[2] Elsewhere he insists that many who understand Greek and Latin are ignorant of their mother-tongue, and that there is little chance for an English poet to acquire and appreciate the delicacies of the English language

without the help of a liberal education, long reading, and digesting of those few good authors we have amongst us, the knowledge of men and manners, the freedom of habitudes and conversation with the best company of both sexes; and, in short, without wearing off the rust which he contracted while he was laying in a stock of learning.[3]

A poet, Addison told the readers of the *Spectator*, 'should take as much pains in forming his imagination, as a philosopher in cultivating his understanding'. For pastoral poetry he will require some knowledge of country life and the works of nature.

If he would go beyond pastoral, and the lower kinds of poetry, he ought to acquaint himself with the pomp and magnificence of courts. He should be very well versed in everything that is noble and stately in the productions of art, whether it appear in painting or statuary, in the great works of architecture which are in their present glory, or in the ruins of those which flourished in former ages.[4]

Johnson's Imlac has similar large demands to make. 'To a poet

---

[1] *Works*, ed. Sir Walter Scott, 1808, xv. 411.
[2] *Essays*, i. 106 f.
[3] Ibid. i. 253.                          [4] *Spectator*, No. 417, 28 June 1712.

nothing can be useless'; the poet must 'store his mind with inexhaustible variety'.[1] In the same spirit Reynolds repeatedly advised the young artist to 'amass a stock of ideas', to prepare his mind by 'laying in proper materials' and to see that it was 'continually fertilized and enriched by foreign matter'. 'Nothing can come of nothing', he warned his students.

The greatest natural genius cannot subsist on its own stock: he who resolves never to ransack any mind but his own, will soon be reduced, from mere barrenness, to the poorest of all imitations; he will be obliged to imitate himself.[2]

All through our period, then, the consensus of opinion is that the poet must be an educated man, well read, far travelled, accustomed to the best society. The list of requirements might be considerably extended, but it will be enough here to mention one more: the poet should know the Rules. In the *Dunciad* there is a contemptuous note on James Ralph:

This low writer . . . was wholly illiterate,[3] and knew no language, not even French. Being advised to read the rules of dramatick poetry before he began a play, he smiled and reply'd, *Shakespeare writ without rules*.[4]

In poetry and drama Pope found a growing number of those upstarts who 'writ without rules', and he resented their intrusion into polite letters. He saw in them a threat to the whole tradition of literary culture that he and his friends represented. His opposition to the Ralphs, therefore, resembled that of the registered practitioner to the chiropractors: such men had not taken the recognized training, they had not graduated.

To Hobbes, writing in 1675, it seemed self-evident that the 'readers of poesie' are 'commonly persons of the best quality'.[5] The spread of education to all classes of society, more especially in the present century, may tend to conceal from us the chasm that yawned two hundred years ago between the educated and the uneducated. They spoke a different language. They still do, but the number of the educated is much larger. In commending the ballad of 'Chevy Chase' to the sympathetic

---

[1] *Rasselas*, ch. x.  [2] *Discourses*, pp. 13, 15, 24, 82.
[3] Cf. Lord Chesterfield, cited in *O.E.D.*: 'The word *illiterate*, in its common acceptation, means a man who is ignorant of those two languages [Greek and Latin].'
[4] *The Dunciad* (1729), iii. 159 n. For the Rules, see pp. 120 ff.
[5] 'Preface to Homer's *Odysses*', Spingarn, ii. 68.

attention of his readers, Addison had argued that human
nature was the same in all reasonable creatures, 'and whatever
falls in with it, will meet with admirers among readers of all
qualities and conditions'. He then proceeds to cite the 'little
old woman' to whom Molière used to read his comedies, and
whose reactions were always confirmed by the polite when the
play was performed.[1] To this specious argument John Dennis
replied that the taste of Molière's old woman was really beside
the point. She might, indeed, have a true taste for comedy,
since comedy is 'an imitation of human nature depraved'; but
we should hardly care to accept her as a judge of poetry. 'What
can be more absurd than to conclude, that because the rabble,
that is, such as never had any education, are tolerable judges
of human nature depraved, that therefore they are judges of
human nature exalted, of which none can be judges but they
who have had the best education?' Addison had thought to
propitiate his polite readers by suggesting a resemblance between

> The hounds ran swiftly thro' the wood
>   The nimble deer to take,
> And with their cries the hills and dales
>   An eccho shrill did make.

and Virgil's

> ———vocat ingenti clamore Cithaeron
> Taygetique canes, domitrixque Epidaurus equorum
> Et vox assensu nemorum ingeminata remugit.

But Dennis appealed equally confidently to *his* polite readers:
'What is there in the first but what is vile and trivial? What
ploughman, what tinker, what trull is not capable of saying the
like?'[2]

Some fifty years later the same point of view was expressed,
but rather more soberly, by Shenstone. In his essay 'On the
Test of Popular Opinion' he introduces to us a citizen, a courtier, and an academic. The citizen says that he hears a lot of talk
about taste, refinement, and politeness,

but methinks the vulgar and illiterate generally approve the same
productions with the connoisseurs. One rarely finds a landskip, a
building, or a play that has charms for the critick exclusive of the
mechanick.

[1] *Spectator*, Nos. 70, 74 (21, 25 May, 1711).
[2] *Critical Works*, ii. 30, 37.

To this the courtier replies that he cannot answer for every individual instance, 'but I think, moderately speaking, the vulgar are generally in the wrong'. He meets the argument that the vulgar find the same beauties in poetry as the man of reading with a flat denial.

Now half or more of the beauties of poetry depend on metaphor or allusion, neither of which by a mind uncultivated can be applied to their proper counterparts. Their beauty of consequence is like a picture to a blind man. How many of these peculiarities in poetry turn upon a knowledge of philosophy and history; and let me add these latent beauties give the most delight to such as can unfold them.

The academic, with characteristic timidity, takes up a middle position, but in the main he sides with the courtier. An author, he thinks,

should not flatter himself with a confused expectation of pleasing both the vulgar and the polite: few things, in comparison, being capable of doing both in any great degree.

His finest things will probably 'escape the organs' of the mob, but he will find his reward in the praise of the discriminating (the 'judicious few'), and in due course the few will impose their values on the many.[1]

Most eighteenth-century critics would have agreed with the courtier and the academic. In that aristocratic age it seemed almost self-evident that 'opinions, like fashions, always descend from those of quality to the middle sort, and thence to the vulgar'.[2] But whether innate or acquired, taste had to be cultivated. A true taste in poetry involved wide general reading, for (as Shenstone's courtier said) it was upon allusion and reference that the contemporary poets depended for most of their overtones. It is frequently suggested by critics that the poetry of Dryden and Pope is too much a poetry of plain statement, and that the denotation of words is for them more important than the connotation. This may be true (but only to a limited extent) of the way in which individual words were used, but behind the surface statement there are often layers of literary or historical reference. When, for instance, Dryden brought his alteration of *The Tempest* upon the stage in 1667,

[1] *The Works in Verse and Prose of William Shenstone, Esq.*, 1764, ii. 8–11.
[2] Swift, *An Argument against Abolishing Christianity.*

his Prologue contained a reference which could hardly be
intelligible to anyone who had not read Shakespeare's play:

> But Shakespear's magick could not copy'd be;
> Within that circle none durst walk but he.

The imaginative identification of Shakespeare with his own
Prospero, suggested by the circle drawn by magicians when they
cast a spell, gives a delicate 'turn' to the thought. The poetry
of Dryden and Pope is full of such confident yet subtle suggestion. How far the allusive habit had entered into the mind of
the age may be seen from a characteristic reflection of Shenstone's on gardens. After remarking on the advantage enjoyed
by some Italian noblemen and gentlemen whose estates are
situated 'on ground mentioned in the classicks', he continues:

> And, even in England, wherever a park or garden happens to
> have been the scene of any event in history, one would surely avail
> one's self of that circumstance, to make it more interesting to the
> imagination. Mottoes should allude to it, columns, etc. record it;
> verses moralize upon it; and curiosity receive it's share of pleasure.[1]

## IV

What, then, are we to conclude about the relationship of the
poet to his readers in the eighteenth century? Are we to assume
that he was quite out of touch with his unlearned readers? In
a more democratic or less scholarly age would they have found
poets to express their deepest thoughts and feelings in language
that all might understand? In view of the esoteric poetry now
being written by many poets in the less scholarly and more
democratic twentieth century, it would be rash to make any
such assumption. Yet it has often been suggested that in the
time of Pope the hungry sheep looked up and were not fed.
Pope and his contemporaries have been accused of cultivating
poetry for a small and exclusive clique. 'Poetry was in the hands
of a few', we are told, 'who kept it within the limits of their
narrow interests; it was poetry in a park surrounded by high
walls. The people were ignored, not admitted.'[2] If this is so,
the people must have made a habit of climbing the walls: few
poets have been read and admired by so large a proportion of
their fellow countrymen as was Pope in his own day. It is true

---

[1] *Works*, ed. cit. ii. 128.
[2] Stopford Brooke, *Naturalism in English Poetry*, 1920, p. 8 f.

that his poetry was fully intelligible only to men and women who had reached a certain level of education; but that was well understood at the time, and the contemporary reader, looking on poetry as a special sort of pleasure which demanded from him a special sort of awareness, was at some pains to equip himself for the enjoyment of it. The demands made upon his literary knowledge differed from poem to poem: at one extreme was Gray's *Elegy*, in which the field of reference was tolerably familiar to the common reader, and at the other, 'The Bard' and 'The Progress of Poesy', which most of Gray's contemporaries, with some justification, found dreadfully obscure. But there is little evidence to show that the eighteenth-century reader was disappointed with the poetry which his poets were providing. As the century advanced, taste was modified in a variety of ways, the range of sensibility shifted slightly, new types of experience were desired; but the poets on the whole seem to have kept in touch with their readers. The notion of a parched and thirsty nation waiting eagerly for the prophet Wordsworth to smite the rock and let forth the living water is at variance with the facts. Wordsworth had first to persuade the public that it was thirsty before he could get it to drink his pure mountain streams at all.

# POETRY IN A POLITE SOCIETY: RESTRAINT

I

To say that eighteenth-century poetry was patronized for the most part by the upper classes of society is to say less than enough to account for its predominantly aristocratic tone. A really extensive middle-class public for poetry can hardly be said to have existed in England until the days of Tennyson and Browning. If we go back to the seventeenth century, and still more to the sixteenth, the reading public grows steadily smaller, while the proportion of readers belonging to the upper class correspondingly increases. Yet the poetry of Donne and Herbert, of Jonson and Drayton, while not noticeably the expression of a middle-class mind, does not give the impression of being addressed to the upper-class reader, or for that matter to any specific reader at all. Why, then, does the upper class exert so marked a pressure on the writers and artists of the eighteenth century?

The explanation is to be found in a new and closer relationship between the writer and his patrons. In the years that followed the Restoration the English upper class was much better organized for the task of keeping itself amused and supporting 'le pénible fardeau de n'avoir rien à faire' than it had ever been before. The great landowners still had their noble mansions in the country, and still passed a few months of the summer there; but the lords and the country gentlemen were beginning to spend more of their time in London, for long the great centre of culture and fashionable amusement, but never more so than since the Restoration. This movement into Town had not perhaps reached its full significance until the 1670s and 1680s, when London was being rebuilt after the Great Fire. Writing in 1667 Thomas Sprat could still say of the French that 'their nobility live commonly close together in their cities, and ours for the most part scattered in their country houses'.[1] But even in 1667 there was a 'season', when Parliament and the law courts were sitting, when the two theatres were open and the places of resort were crowded by men and

[1] Spingarn, ii. 112.

women of fashion. Out of the season society still kept together at Bath, Tonbridge, and the other spas and seaside resorts which were one by one coming into prominence. Society, in fact, was more compact, more conscious of itself than it had been in Elizabethan or Jacobean days. This new gregariousness is reflected in the vastly increased number of eating-houses, and of the comparatively new coffee-houses and chocolate-houses, some of which (like Will's, and, a little later, Button's) were the recognized haunts of literary men. Conversation, that most social of all the arts, was cultivated there, and the discussion of new books and new authors proceeded at different levels of urbanity and wit. After the Restoration, too, the men of letters appear to have enjoyed increased opportunities of mixing on easy terms with the aristocracy. Dryden and Shadwell, Wycherley and Congreve, Swift and Pope and Gay, were all familiar with some of the great noblemen of their day, who were often amateurs of letters themselves.

For a proper understanding of the eighteenth century we should never forget the value then placed upon good conversation. This was the most universal of all the arts, cultivated by all but the most boorish. The writers are never tired of discussing it. Steele gives much of his space in *Tatlers*, *Spectators*, and *Guardians* to explaining the nature and significance of polite conversation; Swift satirizes conversational clichés; Fielding writes a long essay and Cowper a long poem on conversation; Johnson deals with it in the *Rambler* and practises it continually, while Boswell and others record it; Jane Austen counts it among the essential qualifications of a hero or heroine. Whatever the Englishman may have been in the seventeenth century or was to become in the nineteenth and twentieth, there can be no question that in the eighteenth century he was a person of genuinely sociable habits; and the high value placed upon the art of polite conversation is the clearest indication of it. As he became more and more urban, the Englishman grew a little more urbane. 'We polish one another', Shaftesbury had noticed in 1709, 'and rub off our corners and rough sides by a sort of *amicable collision*.'[1]

The art of polite conversation, then, was the special grace of the lady and gentleman; it depended upon the finest qualities of intelligence and character. Restraint, propriety, an absence

---

[1] *Characteristics*, i. 49.

of emphasis, consideration for others and the desire to give them pleasure, a willingness to subordinate what is merely personal or private or a matter of 'self-expression' in favour of what is generally interesting and universally intelligible in polite society, a sense of proportion, the avoidance of mere display, the conscious imitation of the best models (in this case the conversation of the fine lady and the fine gentleman)—these are some of the qualities of good conversation as the eighteenth century understood and practised it. They are also the qualities of the best eighteenth-century architecture, and they are everywhere present in its most characteristic prose. They are also, to a remarkable extent, the qualities of its most characteristic poetry. The poetry of that century, however remote its diction may sometimes be from the idiom of contemporary speech, has at least this in common with conversation that it is consciously addressed to someone else. The eighteenth-century poet is addressing the reader in a variety of ways, and with different ends in view, but he is not murmuring to himself alone. Poetry was to him, like good conversation, a social activity; it exacted from him a consideration for the reader and a corresponding restraint upon himself.

II

Social intercourse would be almost impossible if the individuals forming a society were not willing to accept certain restrictions on their freedom of expression. In dress, behaviour, conversation, and 'all the little intercourses of life', as Steele insists, 'there is a certain deference due to custom; and . . . a man ought to sacrifice his private inclinations and opinions to the practice of the public'.[1] No doubt our manners to-day are a good deal freer than those of the upper classes in the eighteenth century; yet even to-day most people adjust themselves, whether consciously or not, to the company in which they find themselves. But society would become excessively tedious if there were no nonconformists, no eccentrics. Dr. Johnson's reputation in the eighteenth century as a formidable talker was partly due to his habit in a conventional and artificial age of being remarkably unconventional. He resented any doubts being cast on his good manners, but it is clear that he sometimes

---

[1] *Spectator*, No. 576, 4 Aug. 1714.

offended against the contemporary standards of politeness. You never could tell what he would say next, and polite society can only survive on the understanding that truth will not be pursued too eagerly into awkward places. Johnson's conversation was not, in fact, wholly characteristic of his century; the measure of his originality as a talker is that he continually overstepped the limitations that Lord Chesterfield accepted with habitual self-control. How severe those restraints could be may be seen from the kind of advice that Lord Chesterfield used to give his son. He went so far as to warn the boy against laughing:

> Having mentioned laughing, I must particularly warn you against it: and I could heartily wish that you may often be seen to smile, but never heard to laugh while you live. Frequent and loud laughter is the characteristic of folly and ill manners: it is the manner in which the mob express their silly joy at silly things; and they call it being merry. In my mind there is nothing so illiberal and so ill bred, as audible laughter. . . . I am neither of a melancholy, nor a cynical disposition, and am as willing, and as apt, to be pleased as anybody; but I am sure that, since I had the full use of reason, nobody has ever heard me laugh.[1]

Behind Chesterfield's advice to his son, here and elsewhere, lies his consciousness of that society in which all our actions are mirrored. We are in the presence of others, and we must act accordingly.

If Johnson was occasionally hurried into an extravagance of thought or a violence of expression it was when he was carried away by the excitement of conversation; it did not happen in his poetry. His poetry was more deliberately submitted to the public. The eighteenth-century poet's consciousness of this public inhibited the expression of emotion, unless it was of a recognized and acceptable kind.[2] It is absurd to contend that eighteenth-century poetry is lacking in feeling; it is still more naïve to suppose that the poets of that century did not feel as men. Nothing had happened to England or to Englishmen that prevented them feeling the loss of a wife or a child with as much intensity as Englishmen in the reign of Queen Elizabeth or Queen Victoria; nothing had intervened to prevent them from delighting in a warm spring day or from falling in love or from

[1] *Letters*, ed. Bonamy Dobrée, 1932, iii. 1115 f. (9 Mar. 1748).
[2] See Note E, p. 168.

looking back with regret on their lost youth.  They felt such
things as those, and much more, but they rarely gave *direct*
expression to such feelings in their poetry.  Certain more public
emotions, such as the love of country or the sense of national
grief at the death of some illustrious soldier or statesman, they
found little difficulty in expressing adequately.  But it is clear
that the more private and personal emotions aroused a certain
self-consciousness; a man kept those to himself, or unburdened
his soul only to a friend.  It is not therefore an eighteenth-
century poet who writes:

> But she is in her grave, and, oh,
>     The difference to me!

or

> 'O mercy!' to myself I cried,
> 'If Lucy should be dead!'

Such revelations of feeling would have seemed to the eighteenth
century altogether too naïve.  Wordsworth's poems, in fact,
made their way very slowly into public favour in the face of
a criticism that complained of their silliness and childishness.
Francis Jeffrey in particular, doggedly upholding the standards
of the eighteenth century at a time when they were gradually
beginning to disintegrate, puts perhaps more clearly than it had
ever been put before a view of poetry that his own father and
grandfather would certainly have endorsed.  In all large and
polished societies, he tells his readers, there is such a thing as a
general taste.  There is, too, 'a certain tact, which informs us
at once that many things, which we still love and are moved by
in secret, must necessarily be despised as childish, or derided as
absurd'.  In this tact he finds Wordsworth woefully deficient.

If Mr. Wordsworth, instead of confining himself almost entirely
to the society of the dalesmen and cottagers, and little children, who
form the subjects of his book, had condescended to mingle a little
more with the people that were to read and judge of it, we cannot
help thinking that its texture might have been considerably improved.[1]

There, unflinchingly expressed, is the attitude of the eighteenth
century to the poet and his poetry.  The poet's readers are men
and women who have arrived at a certain standard of culture,
and it is a culture of an urban and aristocratic kind; they have

---

[1] *Jeffrey's Essays from 'The Edinburgh Review'*, ed. cit., p. 529 f.

certain well-defined interests, a characteristic (and, though they do not know this, peculiar) mode of thinking and feeling, and when they read poetry they expect a specific kind of pleasure and no other. Their way of thinking is not that of a Covent Garden porter or a Cumberland shepherd; but they, after all—and not the porter or the shepherd—are the readers of poetry, and until they change their nature 'it will remain the poet's office to proceed upon that state of association which actually exists as *general*'.[1] The readers of poetry (in Jeffrey's words, the people who are 'to read and judge of it') are accustomed to a certain reticence in the expression of all feeling, and to a complete silence about some feelings which it is not considered proper to disclose to the world at large. How heavily eighteenth-century manners weighed upon some of the more impulsive souls of the period may be seen from a characteristic outburst of Rousseau's:

In our day, now that more subtle study and a more refined taste have reduced the art of pleasing to a system, there prevails in modern manners a servile and deceptive conformity; so that one would think every mind had been cast in the same mould. Politeness requires this thing; decorum that; ceremony has its forms, and fashion its laws, and these we must always follow, never the promptings of our own nature.

And he continues:

We no longer dare seem what we really are, but lie under a perpetual restraint; in the meantime the herd of men, which we call society, all act under the same circumstances exactly alike, unless very particular and powerful motives prevent them.[2]

If Rousseau were to return to-day he would find less ground for complaint; he might conceivably feel embarrassed at the length to which the twentieth-century writer is prepared to go in exposing to the public his most private thoughts and feelings. That there are still some limits recognized may be deduced from the embarrassment that most people feel when confronted in a railway carriage or a restaurant by some stranger who insists on confessing his sins. But in literature we have grown accustomed to almost every kind of self-display. This breaking down of the once solid barriers between public and private life

[1] *Biographia Literaria*, ii. 104 f.
[2] *A Discourse on the Arts and Sciences*, 1750 (*The Social Contract and Discourses . . .*, trs. G. D. H. Cole, p. 132).

(the process has not yet been carried so far in Europe as in
America) is one of the reasons why eighteenth-century poetry
is apt to seem deficient in feeling and intimacy to the modern
reader.  He misses the personal note with which he has nowadays grown so familiar.  When Gray writes an ode 'On a Distant
Prospect of Eton College' there is no direct expression of his
feelings, except in the second stanza:

> Ah happy hills, ah pleasing shade,
> Ah fields belov'd in vain,
> Where once my careless childhood stray'd,
> A stranger yet to pain!

Yet the whole poem is about Gray's feelings, a Gray who has
already experienced the vicissitudes of life, and who now feels
as a man what, as a schoolboy at Eton, he had only construed—
'Sunt lacrimae rerum et mentem mortalia tangunt'.  But Gray
is an artist of exquisite restraint; his feelings steal upon us imper-
ceptibly as he recalls, but hardly seeks to individualize, particular experiences:

> Who foremost now delight to cleave
> With pliant arm thy glassy wave?
> The captive linnet which enthrall?

Gray never walks boldly up to the front door and rattles on the
knocker.  His personal feeling is almost never stated, it emerges;
and the eighteenth century liked him the better for it.[1]

Naturally enough men and women could not always live up
to those severe standards even in the eighteenth century; and
among the novelists Fielding delighted, with a humanity which
seemed to Richardson perverse and 'low', to depict those
moments of crisis when all restraint is thrown aside.  But a poet
could not decently plead overpowering feelings as an excuse
for some emotional indiscretion *in print*.  Whatever he might be
driven to write in the warmth or hurry of feeling, there was no
compulsion on him to publish it in cold blood.  It is significant
that some of Johnson's most personal poems were written, not
in English but in Latin: the dead language was almost a cipher
by means of which he could express himself more freely and
frankly than he would have cared to do in English.  Nor did he
think of publishing those poems; he was writing for himself
alone.

[1] See Note F, p. 169.

So little was the eighteenth-century poet habituated to the free expression of spontaneous emotions that when a writer like Edward Young attempts to 'give a loose' to feeling in his *Night Thoughts*, we are apt to-day to doubt his sincerity and deplore his exhibitionism. We feel almost as if we had come unawares upon the poet in his underclothes; there is nothing to be done but close the door and tiptoe away as softly as possible. What came naturally enough to Wordsworth was difficult and even embarrassing to the eighteenth-century poet: if one has grown accustomed, like public-school boys, to conceal rather than express the feelings it becomes more and more troublesome to express them naturally and without self-consciousness. It was therefore *natural* for Gray to write impersonally about 'the wretch' who long had tossed on the thorny bed of pain, and to express his sense of returning vitality through the discoveries of this anonymous convalescent:

> The meanest flowret of the vale,
> The simplest note that swells the gale,
> The common Sun, the air, the skies,
> To him are opening Paradise.

It would have been unnatural for Wordsworth to write on such impersonal terms. He would have written in the first person, speaking either for himself, or more probably, perhaps, for some aged cottager—simple, garrulous, and direct, using the language really spoken by men:

> Oh Sir! I get about a bit,
>    I see the blessed sun on high;
> And I must think, do all I can,
>    'Tis Paradise in yon blue sky.

Wordsworth's poetry continually takes the form of a personal statement of what he had thought or felt ('And much it grieved my heart to think . . .'; 'And, oh, the difference to me!'; 'My heart leaps up when I behold . . .'; 'I thought of Chatterton, the marvellous boy'; 'Ne'er saw I, never felt, a calm so deep!'): Gray's poetry is almost uniformly impersonal. But the difference is not one of feeling and not-feeling; it is a difference mainly in the conventions of expression, which turns ultimately on a different relationship with the reader.

A curious and interesting example of the eighteenth-century expression of feeling is the poem which Lord Lyttelton wrote

to the memory of his first wife, who died in childbed. There
can be no doubt about the sincerity of his grief, as those who
read the poem in the *Oxford Book of Eighteenth Century Verse* will
readily agree. The poem opens in a vein of unforced simplicity,
which would be the natural expression of sorrow in any age.

> In vain I look around
> O'er the well-known ground,
> My Lucy's wonted footsteps to descry;
> Where oft we us'd to walk,
> Where oft in tender talk
> We saw the summer sun go down the sky;
> Nor by yon fountain's side,
> Nor where its waters glide
> Along the valley, can she now be found:
> In all the wide-stretch'd prospect's ample bound
> No more my mournful eye
> Can aught of her espy,
> But the sad sacred earth where her dear relics lie.

But the Oxford editor has given us the poem that Lyttelton
should have written, not the one that he actually wrote. After
two more stanzas in the same strain (his Lucy preferred the
quiet retirement of Hagley to the glitter of courts; she devoted
herself to her children, guiding their infant steps; how will the
unhappy father, alone and oppressed with his griefs, bring up
those infants without her?) Lyttelton suddenly breaks out into:

> Where were ye, Muses, when relentless Fate
> From these fond arms your fair disciple tore?

and in succeeding stanzas we meet with 'Castalia's plain', 'the
Thespian vallies', 'Mincio's bank', Petrarch and his Laura, and
much else. All this the Oxford editor judiciously omits, together
with the most purple of all Lyttelton's patches, the stanza of
the orange-tree:

> So where the silent streams of Liris glide,
> In the soft bosom of Campania's vale,
> When now the wintry tempests all are fled,
> And genial Summer breathes her gentle gale,
> The verdant orange lifts its beauteous head:
> From every branch the balmy flowerets rise,
> On every bough the golden fruits are seen;
> With odours sweet it fills the smiling skies,
> The wood-nymphs tend it, and th' Idalian queen.

But in the midst of all its blooming pride,
A sudden blast from Apenninus blows,
   Cold with perpetual snows:
The tender blighted plant shrinks up its leaves, and dies.

Towards the close Lyttelton returns to his earlier and happier manner:

O best of wives! O dearer far to me
   Than when thy virgin charms
   Were yielded to my arms,
How can my soul endure the loss of thee?
How in the world, to me a desart grown,
   Abandon'd and alone,
Without my sweet companion can I live? . . .[1]

Two voices are there in this monody: one giving us the natural unaffected melody that corresponds to Lyttelton's real feelings, the other supplying the sort of orchestration that an eighteenth-century poet considered proper. Among contemporary comments on the poem, two may be cited for the light they throw on eighteenth-century taste. 'If it were all like the fourth stanza,' Gray wrote to Horace Walpole, 'I should be excessively pleased. Nature and sorrow, and tenderness, are the true genius of such things; and something of these I find in several parts of it (not in the orange-tree): poetical ornaments are foreign to the purpose, for they only shew a man is not sorry.'[2] Gray's attitude here is the same as Johnson's on similar occasions, and it would probably be endorsed by most readers of poetry to-day. But to Lyttelton's friend, Dr. Philip Doddridge, it was the simplicity that let the poem down, and the orange-tree stanza that was most admirable. In replying to Doddridge's criticism, Lyttelton not unnaturally defended both simplicity and orange-tree.

Simplicity [he argues] if it does not descend into *vulgarism*, is the chief excellence of all kinds of writing, but above all of those in which the heart is to speak. Without the utmost simplicity, both of thought and diction, the *pathos* cannot be preserved; and I would admit no ornaments into such a work, but merely as pauses at proper intervals, to relieve the reader from the emotions of grief,

---

[1] Chalmers, xiv. 180 ff. Mr. Norman Callan has drawn my attention to an echo of Pope (*Iliad* i; Chalmers, xix. 14):
   Not half so dear were Clytæmnestra's charms,
   When first her blooming beauties blest my arms.
[2] *Correspondence*, i. 288 f.

which are excited by the more passionate parts. In those parts, figures, or metaphors, or any high colouring, or hardness of style, are quite improper; and points, or *concetti*, are insupportable faults, however witty and brilliant they may be. . . .[1]

As for the orange-tree, the 'high colouring' of that simile would have been 'very improper in those [parts] where grief alone could find room to speak'.

How little eighteenth-century poetry was 'the spontaneous overflow of powerful feelings' may be guessed from an unlucky episode in the poetical career of Pope. In the summer of 1718 he was staying at Stanton Harcourt as the guest of Lord Harcourt. One day a thunderstorm broke over the district, and Lord Harcourt's servants, who were haymaking at the time, scattered in all directions to seek shelter. Among them were two young lovers, John Hewet and Sarah Drew—two names very common in the Berkshire villages to this day. Sarah was terrified and sank down on a haycock, and her lover hurriedly raked together some heaps of hay to cover her, and then lay down beside her. The thunder rolled, the lightning flashed; and when the storm had blown over the other labourers came out to look for John and Sarah. They found John Hewet with one arm about his Sarah's neck, as if to screen her from the lightning. But both of them were dead. There was no mark or discolouring on either of them, except that Sarah's eyebrows were a little singed, and there was a small spot between her breasts. This sad event so preyed on the poet's mind (as well it might) that he told the story, quite unaffectedly and with genuine concern, to several different correspondents, and—what was quite unusual for him—set himself almost immediately to mourn the event in verse. The situation with which he had to deal was one that Wordsworth would have had no difficulty in handling; it was the perfect theme for a lyrical ballad. But for Pope it was not nearly so easy; indeed, it was the wrong material altogether. He did not attempt to present the death of the lovers as a moving accident, and still less as an experience that had come to *him*. Instead, he suggested to Lord Harcourt that he should erect a monument to the memory of the unhappy lovers, and himself set about writing their epitaph. The result, to say the least of it, was not a triumph for decorum:

[1] Rose Mary Davis, *The Good Lord Lyttelton*, 1939, p. 138.

When Eastern lovers feed the fun'ral fire,
On the same pile their faithful fair expire:
Here pitying Heav'n that virtue mutual found,
And blasted both, that it might neither wound.
Hearts so sincere th' Almighty saw well pleas'd,
Sent his own lightning, and the victims seiz'd.

To this Pope added gallantly in a letter to Lady Mary Wortley Montagu:

The greatest honour people of this low degree could have was to be remembered on a little monument; unless you will give them another, —that of being honoured with a tear from the finest eyes in the world.[1]

An epitaph is not (or certainly was not with Pope) a cry of the heart, and it would be unfair to blame Pope for not giving what he never intended to give. But we could hardly find a better example of the way in which the raw materials of human experience were habitually transmuted in eighteenth-century poetry. A Burns, a Blake, a Wordsworth constantly succeed to a remarkable degree in finding the words that will enable them to hand on their experience to the reader, who re-experiences it in all its original freshness. Pope's epitaph, though it had its origin in a genuine and moving experience, is not intended to be a mere statement of it, but a decorative rendering of it, or, more accurately, of ideas arising from it. The sharp impact of the experience has been lost; indeed, it has never been desired. Pope's own feelings have been decently veiled; he has concentrated on the memorial. The event and its accompanying emotions have been formalized and made impersonal to the poet. But that, of course, is what the polite reader of the period wanted. He had no desire for naked experience; about *that* he felt much as the lady in the stage-coach did about Joseph Andrews: 'O J—sus! A naked man! Dear coachman, drive on and leave him.'

This sort of preference is one of the most difficult things for the modern reader to understand, let alone to accept or enjoy. What is characteristically absent from eighteenth-century poetry (and, indeed, from all the arts of the period) is the sense of immediate, direct contact with experience. Eighteenth-century poetry had almost always been submitted to a process in the poet's mind analogous to what went on in the kitchen

[1] *Works*, ed. Elwin–Courthope, ix. 399.

before dinner was served in the dining-room.  Mr. Knightley's dislike of picnics is characteristic of the whole century.  *His* idea of the simple and natural, it will be recalled, was 'to have the table spread in the dining-room.  The nature and the simplicity of gentlemen and ladies, with their servants and furniture, . . . is best observed by meals within doors.'  The reader of poetry in Mr. Knightley's day liked his poetry that way too.

To Wordsworth, on the other hand, the important thing is always the experience in all its original purity.  If his poem is successful he has made us feel exactly what he himself felt at the time: the very wind of it passes across our brow, the taste of it is on our lips.  Like the strawberries that poor Mrs. Elton wanted to pick ('we are to walk about your gardens, and gather the strawberries ourselves, and sit under trees; . . . it is to be all out of doors') the experience in each poem of Wordsworth's is fresh and unspoilt; it has not been fingered, nothing has been 'done' to it.

To see Wordsworth at work we could not do better than turn to 'The Idiot Boy', where he is transmitting an imaginative experience in all its uniqueness and unexpectedness: what it feels like to be an idiot boy riding on a pony in bright moonlight; what it feels like to be a mother who has lost her idiot son—the whole palpitating, bewildering, agonizing experience of a rather weak-witted woman driven nearly crazy by the loss of her child.  Almost everything is seen from the point of view of the idiot ('But when the pony *moved his legs* . . .'), or from the standpoint of the distracted mother:

> She looks again—her arms are up—
> She screams—she cannot move for joy. . . .

These astonishing lines have all the force of a primitive painting: human action and human passion have been reduced to their simplest terms.  Sometimes the experience comes to us from neither mother nor son.  The stillness of the night, the silent town with the moon riding high above it in the blue sky, the queer hush before dawn—

> The streams with softest sound are flowing,
> The grass you almost hear it growing—

the hooting of the owlets, the little birds beginning to stir sleepily in the hedgerows, the gradual fading of the moon ('so pale you scarcely looked at her'), the return of the travellers to their cottage: everything is given with a remarkable directness that even Wordsworth never surpassed.

In Donne's poem 'The Calme' or in Coleridge's 'Frost at Midnight' we again meet with an experience just as sharply individualized, and one from which (as with 'The Idiot Boy') the original glow and colour have not departed. Why do we so rarely find anything comparable in the poetry of the eighteenth century? The answer, it has already been suggested, can scarcely be that the poets of that century never had such matters to express. To suppose so is to postulate a quite unprecedented break in the continuity of human experience. Even if we committed ourselves to so rash a theory the poets themselves would disprove it, since they occasionally give us poems, like Ambrose Philips's 'Winter Piece', of the kind in question. Normally, however, they drew a clear distinction between what they considered to be private and what could be made public, what was merely a matter of personal memoranda and what might be worked into a regular poem.[1] That some such distinction was widely accepted, and that it was not peculiar to the poets, may be seen from the remarkable sketches of nature made by Gainsborough, but made by him as private records for his own use. In those sketches, so obviously dashed off at speed, Gainsborough seized with remarkable intimacy the momentary appearance, the atmosphere of a sunny morning, the look of the wind passing through a clump of trees. But a picture was another thing altogether: *that* was a work of art, based on the recollection of many sunny mornings and many wind-swept clumps of trees. In the finished picture the sense of immediacy has largely disappeared; instead, many separate observations and much artistic experience are blended into one harmonious composition. It is much the same with the poet Gray. What he wrote in his *Journal* was for his own eye, and what he wrote in letters to his friends was for their eyes alone; in both journal and letters he is far freer and far closer to the momentary appearance of things and to the thoughts and feelings that take shape in his consciousness as he writes than he ever cared to be in his poetry. It is significant that when his friend Mason came to publish Gray's letters he felt compelled to prepare them for the public. It was never his intention to present the public

[1] See Note G, p. 169.

with Gray's letters (private letters, not written for publication) exactly as they stood. 'I will promise my reader', he said, 'that he shall, in the following pages, seldom behold Mr. Gray in any light than that of a scholar and poet'[1]—the very light, in fact, in which Gray had always presented himself to the public, in so far as he had ever allowed himself to publish what he had written. He therefore prepared the letters for publication by eliminating Gray's slang, his contractions, and many of his little intimacies and indiscretions. About such editing the twentieth century is apt to express indignation, and many people to-day probably feel that Mason cut out all the most interesting bits; but Mason was publishing a *book*, and he drew the distinction, usual in that century, between what was and what was not fit for the public. Boswell's *Life of Johnson* had not yet appeared to accustom readers to a new range of intimacy; still less Rousseau's *Confessions*. When Boswell's *Life* did appear, its intimacies startled many readers; they startled even Wordsworth. 'The Life of Johnson by Boswell', he wrote, 'had broken through many pre-existing delicacies, and afforded the British public an opportunity of acquiring experience, which before it had happily wanted.'[2] The twentieth-century writer and his readers are scarcely aware of any such inhibitions, and when they meet with restraint and formality in eighteenth-century poetry are too apt to assume a want of feeling or an obtuseness of perception. In an age of publicity we have almost no private life left; the newspaper reporter enters the cottage and the palace, views the body and gets the widow's story, photographs the fatal mansion and marks the window with a cross. Whether we wish to or not, whether we are tender or unfeeling, we are 'condemn'd alike to groan' for the pains of others. But in the eighteenth century this curiosity about what was happening to other people had not yet become intense; men were left to live their own private lives, they were not expected to unbosom their feelings to strangers, they did not obtrude their personal concerns upon society.

In his essay on Gray, Matthew Arnold makes a good deal, after his fashion, of the observation made about Gray by his Swiss friend, Bonstetten: 'He would never talk of himself, never would allow me to speak to him of his poetry. If I quoted lines

---

[1] *The Poems of Mr. Gray . . .*, 1775. See Gray, *Correspondence*, i, p. xiv.
[2] *Wordsworth's Literary Criticism*, p. 208.

to him, he kept silence like an obstinate child.' On which
Arnold reiterates, 'He never spoke out', and goes on to explain
that 'Gray, a born poet, fell upon an age of prose'. The truth
is surely less depressing than that: Gray's misfortune—if it was
a misfortune—was only that he did not fall upon an age of
romantic poetry. A. E. Housman behaved in much the same
way to young men who quoted *A Shropshire Lad* at him—not
because he fell in an age of prose, but because he was an
Englishman and a don, and found it difficult to bring himself to
such intimacies with men much younger than himself.

In his Epitaph on John Hewet and Sarah Drew Pope had
felt very sincerely and expressed his feelings very badly. A far
happier instance of his ability to transmit his feeling is the
'Epistle to Miss Blount on her leaving the Town after the Coro-
nation'. The poet daydreams about his mistress in the country,
confined to the society of 'dull aunts and croaking rooks', and
with nothing whatever to do except

> muse and spill her solitary tea;
> Or o'er cold coffee trifle with the spoon,
> Count the slow clock, and dine exact at noon. . . .

When *she* muses it is of the Town she is thinking, the Corona-
tion celebrations, the lords and earls, the balls and assemblies—
and then, one flirt of her fan and all the vision disappears! But
the poet, too, has his vision as he languishes in the Town:

> So when your slave, at some dear, idle time,
> (Not plagu'd with headachs, or the want of rhime)
> Stands in the streets, abstracted from the crew,
> And while he seems to study, thinks of you:
> Just when his fancy points your sprightly eyes,
> Or sees the blush of *Parthenissa* rise,
> Gay pats my shoulder, and you vanish quite;
> Streets, chairs, and coxcombs, rush upon my sight;
> Vext to be still in town, I knit my brow,
> Look sow'r, and hum a song—as you may now.

Pope can manage his feeling perfectly here, because it never
goes beyond the studied carelessness of fashionable society. It
is what an intelligent young diarist noticed and duly entered
in his diary in the year 1715, after watching some people of
fashion playing at ombre at Lady Pilkington's: 'I don't find
among these fine folks that their conversation is better or more

improving or diverting than others', only they have a certain
genteel way of carrying it and saying very ordinary things
without concern.'[1] But if Pope has caught to perfection this
unconcern of manner, the feeling is there beyond doubt—as
anyone with an ear for rhythm could tell at once. As a love
poem this Epistle of Pope's is a less passionate and a far less
direct expression of feeling than

> I sigh'd, and said amang them a',
>   'Ye are na Mary Morison'—

but it is none the less a love-poem, and there can be little doubt
that the lady, who was well versed in the artificialities of polite
society, had no difficulty whatever in recognizing the accents
of genuine feeling. We must not allow the mothers of idiot boys
to make us suspect the emotions of others more happily placed.

On the other hand, it would be useless to deny that the
eighteenth-century poet generally makes poor work of the
expression of his 'natural' feelings. He can give us 'Sally in our
Alley' and Cowper's 'Lines on the Receipt of his Mother's
Picture', but such poems, if not uncommon, are not very
numerous during the period. Occasionally we get conscious
exercises in feeling. The eighteenth-century poet, *in his character
as a poet*, felt justified in departing very far from the ordinary
prose levels of thought and feeling. Some interesting evidence
on this aspect of the poet's profession comes from Coleridge,
who had a good deal more of the eighteenth century in him
than Wordsworth. In a letter to Southey Coleridge replies to a
request for permission to reprint the 'Monody on the Death of
Chatterton' in a forthcoming edition of Chatterton's poems.
He has been re-reading his own poem, and he has now a poor
opinion of it: the emotion he had felt when he wrote the poem
was genuine enough, but it had hurried him into extravagance
and hyperbole.

A young man by strong feelings is impelled to write on a particular
subject, and this is all his feelings do for him. They set him upon the
business, and then they leave him. He has such a high idea of what
poetry ought to be, that he cannot conceive that such things as his
natural emotions may be allowed to find a place in it; his learning,
therefore, his fancy, or rather conceit, and all his powers of buckram
are put on the stretch.[2]

---

[1] *The Diary of Dudley Ryder, 1715–1716*, ed. W. Matthews, 1939, p. 217.
[2] *Letters of S. T. Coleridge*, ed. E. H. Coleridge, i. 223.

In this devastatingly honest analysis of the 'Monody' Coleridge is, in fact, describing an attitude to poetry which (if kindlier expressed) most eighteenth-century poets would have found little difficulty in accepting. The poets (and their readers) had 'a high idea of what poetry ought to be', and consciously braced themselves at times to what they considered an adequate emotional state. Poetry, said Steele, with the air of a man stating a truism, 'is in itself an elevation above ordinary and common sentiments'.[1] It was not at times the poet's natural feelings as a man that were called into play so much as his elevated emotions as a poet. It was surely something of this sort that happened when Pope wrote *Eloisa to Abelard*: that poem is a conscious exercise in emotional utterance, similar in kind to the passionate monologues in the tragedies of his friend, Nicholas Rowe. In Rowe's tragedy, *The Royal Convert*, Rodogune is in love with Aribert, but Aribert loves Ethelinda. Rodogune is torturing herself with thoughts of her rival.

*Rodogune.*   How is she form'd? With what superior grace,
              This rival of my love? What envious God,
              In scorn of Nature's wretched works below,
              Improv'd and made her more than half divine?
              How has he taught her lips to breathe ambrosia?
              How dy'd her blushes with the morning's red,
              And cloath'd her with the fairest beams of light,
              To make her shine beyond me?

*Aribert.*                                 Spare the theme.[2]

But Rowe cannot afford to spare the theme; he is writing poetic drama, and this is what it required of him in the reign of Queen Anne. The trouble here is not that he is using a poetic diction (there is little of that), but that this highfalutin emotional utterance is what he believes to be proper to tragic drama. Rodogune's speech is over-wrought, over-coloured, remote from natural human expression. Rowe is constantly decorating ideas in this sumptuous fashion; his language has all the pomp of velvet trappings and elaborate folds of drapery. It belongs to the period just as much as the elaborate funeral processions with the mourners following the escutcheoned hearse in their ponderous and ill-sprung coaches.

Feeling such as that expressed by Rowe's Rodogune, rhetorical feeling, is common enough in eighteenth-century tragedy.

[1] *Tatler*, No. 244, 31 Oct. 1710.          [2] IV. I. 175 ff.

It is perhaps to be found at its best just before the century opened, in some of Dryden's Heroic plays. The celebrated passage in *The Indian Emperor* (III. ii) will show how good rhetoric can be at its best:[1]

> All things are hush'd, as Nature's self lay dead;
> The mountains seem to nod their drowsy head;
> The little birds, in dreams, their songs repeat,
> And sleeping flow'rs beneath the night-dew sweat.
> Ev'n Lust and Envy sleep; yet Love denies
> Rest to my soul, and slumber to my eyes.

Such passages as this serve the same purpose, in a more refined form, as the drums and trumpets and the stage battles to which critics of the Heroic Drama took exception; they 'raise the imagination of the audience' and help the dramatist to obtain 'an absolute dominion over the minds of the spectators'.[2] It is not in the nature of rhetoric to be precise; its purpose is to induce an emotional state in the mind of the reader or listener so that certain other more specific purposes may be served. There is little *crude* rhetoric in eighteenth-century poetry. When we do come upon it, as in Young's *Night Thoughts*, we are reading what is essentially a dramatic monologue. Eighteenth-century poetry, though it has normally a rhetorical basis, is usually a good deal quieter and more restrained than Young's; for that consciousness of an audience which encouraged extravagance *in the theatre* had usually the very opposite effect in the poetry of that milder Muse to which most of the poets owed their inspiration.

[1] See Note H, p. 169.          [2] Dryden, *Essays*, i. 154 f.

# V
# REFINEMENT

POLITE society not only exercises certain restraints on its members; it expects certain refinements. These can only be obtained at a cost. Refinement frequently comes into conflict with expressiveness; you must avoid some statements and some expressions because they are too crude, too forthright, because they arouse sensations of disgust. The point at which anything becomes disgusting will vary enormously with different individuals and different nations; it will vary, too, from one century to another, and from one class of society to another.

There can be no question that the formal manners of upper-class society in the eighteenth century were often abnormally fastidious. No doubt the coarseness, both of thought and expression, which becomes immediately apparent in this century as soon as we step among the middle or lower classes had a good deal to do with the exaggerated refinement of polite society. The artificial dikes which had been built to hold back the encroaching flood of vulgarity had to be maintained in strict repair; the muddy boots of the squire, the aroma of stable-dung and tobacco which he brought with him, his horse-laugh and coarse jests, had to be kept out of the drawing-room. Millamant coping distastefully with her country cousin, drunk and boisterous—'Sir Wilfull grows very powerful. Eh! how he smells! I shall be overcome if I stay'—is an epitome of the whole period. Where manners are artificial rather than natural one cannot be too careful, and the more careful one is the greater is the effect of a *faux pas*. In any case the culture of the Millamants and the Mirabells was rarely much more than skin-deep. The century never achieved more than a precarious balance: the second book of the *Dunciad* and some of the verses which Swift allowed himself to write would alone show how precarious it was. The combination of an exquisitely delicate artistry with a coarseness of spiritual fibre is one of the paradoxes of the period. Little wonder, then, that the polite, beset on all sides, were driven in self-protection to an excessive refinement and artificiality which end only too often in a refusal to accept the ordinary facts of existence.

The effect of this upon poetry—and particularly in the first half of the century—is curious. Partly owing to this excessive refinement, and partly to the widespread notion that poetry, like the church service, necessitated a conscious withdrawal from everyday concerns and a certain remoteness from ordinary life, the eighteenth-century poet was often driven to exclude from his poetry much of his normal environment. That could be done, and was done, quite easily; but it necessarily narrowed the range of the instrument on which the poet played and the tunes he might play on it. He was beset by inhibitions, and from a good deal of what was going on in the street or in the human heart he had to avert his eyes.

It was not merely the thought that had to be refined to satisfy the contemporary reader; language, too—the 'dress of thought' —had also to be decontaminated from all mean or vulgar associations. The eighteenth-century point of view on this important matter was put by Addison with his customary lucidity:

If clearness and perspicuity were only to be consulted the poet would have nothing else to do but to clothe his thoughts in the most plain and natural expressions. But, since it often happens that the most obvious phrases, and those which are used in ordinary conversation, become too familiar to the ear, and contract a kind of meanness by passing through the mouths of the vulgar, a poet should take particular care to guard himself against idiomatic ways of speaking.

So far from thinking that it is an advantage to the poet to write in 'a selection of the language really used by men', Addison is of opinion that Homer and Virgil may be counted fortunate to have written their poetry in what are now dead languages:

Were there any mean phrases or idioms in Virgil and Homer, they would not shock the ear of the most delicate modern reader so much as they would have done that of an old Greek or Roman, because we never hear them pronounced in our streets, or in ordinary conversation.[1]

Elsewhere Addison notes that the names of English rivers— because of their familiarity—are less poetical than those of the ancient world; and in his remarks on the ballad of 'Chevy Chase', after quoting two stanzas recounting the deaths of Earl Douglas, Sir Hugh Montgomery, Sir Charles Carrel, Sir

[1] *Spectator*, No. 285, 26 Jan. 1712.

Charles Murrel of Ratcliff, and Sir David Lamb, he observes with entire consistency that 'the familiar sound in these names destroys the majesty of the description'.[1] Three of his own poems, 'The Battle of the Pygmies and Cranes', 'The Barometer', and 'A Bowling-green', are concerned with 'mean' or trivial subjects, and Addison has written them in Latin. Commenting on this, Johnson remarks that 'when the matter is low or scanty a dead language, in which nothing is mean because nothing is familiar, affords great conveniences'.[2] But English poets must, of course, write most of their poetry in English; and since English is not a dead language, Addison and his contemporaries felt that—for epic and certain other kinds of poetry— they had to deaden it or anaesthetize it by suitable injections of words not used in the street or market-place.

In the Postscript to his translation of the *Odyssey* Pope echoes Addison; he, too, seems half to regret that English is not a dead language, but only too disconcertingly alive:

It must also be allowed that there is a majesty and harmony in the Greek language, which greatly contribute to elevate and support the narration. But I must also observe, that this is an advantage grown upon the language since Homer's time: for things are removed from vulgarity by being out of use; and if the words we could find in any present language were equally sonorous or musical in themselves, they would still appear less poetical and uncommon than those of a dead one, from this only circumstance, of being in every man's mouth.[3]

Some thirty years earlier Dryden had also had occasion to remark on the difficulties that beset the poet writing in what was still a living language. Virgil's *mollis amaracus*, for instance; how should a modern English poet translate that sonorous phrase?

If I should translate it *sweet marjoram*, as the word signifies, the reader would think I had mistaken Virgil: for those village words, as I may call them, give us a mean idea of the thing; but the sound of the Latin is so much more pleasing, by the just mixture of the vowels with the consonants, that it raises our fancies to conceive somewhat more noble than a common herb, and to spread roses under him, and strew lilies over him; a bed not unworthy the grandson of the goddess.[4]

Dryden's Venus, therefore, crowns the head of the young Asca-

---

[1] *Spectator*, No. 74, 25 May 1711. See Note I, p. 169.
[2] Johnson, *Lives*, ii. 83.
[3] Chalmers, xix. 279.          [4] *Essays*, ii. 233.

nius with a wreath of myrtle, and softly lays him, not on marjoram, but on 'a flowery bed'. In Dryden's dilemma we can
catch a glimpse of the influence—here, at any rate, a baleful
influence—of constantly reading poetry in a dead language.
The reason that Dryden gives for preferring *mollis amaracus* to
'sweet marjoram' ('the sound of the Latin is so much more
pleasing, by the just mixture of the vowels with the consonants') will scarcely bear examination; the English words
sound as pleasingly in the ear as the Latin. His real reason for
shrinking from 'sweet marjoram' is that it is a 'village word',
and that means, for Dryden, that it is too humble for epic
poetry.[1] Worse still, it brings with it too sharp an air of actuality; it disturbs that calm and remote atmosphere which he
associates with classical poetry. But the calm and the remoteness are at least partly due to the passage of the centuries, and
if Virgil was not afraid of *mollis amaracus* his translator should
not refuse 'sweet marjoram'. The twentieth-century translator
would not hesitate for a moment; it would need something
much more prosaic—like, say, 'bachelor's buttons'—to drive
him to such a periphrasis as 'flowery bed'.

It cannot be denied that eighteenth-century refinement is
often a false and exaggerated refinement, or that the poet and
his readers had an almost morbid dread of mean or ludicrous
associations radiating from the words used in everyday life.[2]
The more poetry refused those everyday words, the greater
was the danger that the unguarded introduction of some quite
natural expression might break the poetical circuit between
poet and reader. To-day—such is the gap between us and the
eighteenth century—the situation is almost completely reversed:
the modern poet must guard himself against 'poetical' words.
But we must accept here a genuine difference of poetical conventions, a difference in the sort of expectations present in the
mind of a reader when he opens a volume of poetry. There is
no lack of evidence as to how the eighteenth century felt in
those matters. In a well-known passage Johnson singles out a
speech of Lady Macbeth's to illustrate the unfortunate effect of
low expressions. After telling us that 'words become low by the

[1] Cf. Boileau's objection to 'village words' (*L'Art poétique*, ii. 17 f.):
            cet autre, abject en son langage,
      Fait parler ses bergers comme on parle au village.
[2] Adam Smith 'could not endure the ballad of "Clym of the Clough" because
the author had not written like a gentleman' (*Wordsworth's Literary Criticism*, p. 6).

occasions to which they are applied, or the general character of
them who use them; and the disgust which they produce arises
from the revival of those images with which they are commonly
united', he proceeds to quote Lady Macbeth's words—

> Come, thick night!
> And pall thee in the dunnest smoke of hell,
> That my keen knife see not the wound it makes;
> Nor heav'n peep through the blanket of the dark,
> To cry, Hold, hold!

To the language of this passage Johnson has three objections
to offer: 'dun' is an epithet 'now seldom heard but in the stable',
'knife' makes him think of butchers, and the expression 'peep
through the blanket' has such a ludicrous sound in his ears that
he can 'scarce check [his] risibility'.[1] We cannot suppose that
Johnson is thinking up those objections to support a thesis:
Shakespeare's language was continually giving such shocks to
a century accustomed to a poetic diction which, like Dante's,
had been passed through a kind of linguistic sieve. A contemporary of Johnson's, the Scottish poet William Hamilton of
Bangour, undertook on one occasion to show what might be
done by way of refining Shakespeare. He chose for his experiment some words uttered by Lear in his agony: 'Thou owest
the worm no silk, the beast no hide, the sheep no wool, the cat
no perfume. . . .' Meditating on this, Hamilton produced his
own version for an age of greater refinement:

> For thee, the skilful worm, of specious hue,
> No shining threads of ductile radiance drew;
> For thee no sun the ripening gem refin'd;
> No bleating innocence the fleece resign'd:
> The hand of luxury ne'er taught to pour
> O'er thy faint limbs the oil's refreshing show'r. . . .[2]

Perhaps the fairest comment on those remarkable lines is a
passage from one of Lord Chesterfield's letters to his son. In
those modern days, he tells the boy, elegance is all:

People know very little of the world, and talk nonsense, when they

---

[1] *Rambler*, No. 168, 26 Oct. 1751.

[2] Chalmers, xv. 624. Cf. James Beattie's 'Song in imitation of Shakespeare's
"Blow, blow, thou winter wind" ' (ibid., xviii. 543):

> Blow, blow, thou vernal gale!
> Thy balm will not avail
> To ease my aching breast. . . .

talk of plainness and solidity unadorned; they will do nothing:
mankind has been long out of a state of nature, and the golden age
of native simplicity will never return.  Whether for the better or the
worse, no matter; but we are refined; and plain manners, plain dress,
and plain diction, would as little do in life, as acorns, herbage, and
the water of the neighbouring spring, would do at table.[1]

Low thoughts and low expressions, then, were to be avoided.
The eighteenth-century poet, writing his own original poetry,
had little difficulty in complying with the taste of the age.  But
when he was translating the poetry of an earlier and less refined
age, he might, as we have seen, encounter serious difficulties.
When Pope undertook to translate the *Odyssey* he secured the
assistance of two friends, Elijah Fenton and the Rev. William
Broome.  On his way through Book XX Fenton ran into trouble,
and wrote to Broome about it:

How I shall get over the bitch and her puppies, the roasting of the
black puddings, as Brault translated it, and the cow-heel that was
thrown at Ulysses' head, I know not.[2]

The bitch that Fenton found to be a poetical liability appears
in a simile near the beginning of the book:

And as a bitch stands over her tender whelps growling, when she sees
a man she does not know, and is eager to fight, so his [*sc.* Ulysses']
heart growled within him. . . .[3]

In his rendering of the passage Fenton avoids the word 'bitch',
but succeeds, by a departure from English idiom, in indicating
the sex; the puppies are generalized, and both the growling
and the person growled at are dignified:

> As o'er her young the mother-mastiff growls,
> And bays the stranger groom: so wrath compress'd,
> Recoiling, mutter'd thunder in his breast. . . .[4]

The cow-heel which Ctesippus flung at the head of Ulysses
presented Fenton with a stiffer problem of devitalization.  This
unheroic action, which took place when the suitors were at
dinner, is described by Homer quite simply and directly:

So saying, he hurled with strong hand the hoof of an ox, taking it up
from the basket where it lay.[5]

[1] *Letters*, ed. Bonamy Dobrée, 1932, v. 2061 (20 Nov. 1753).
[2] *The Works of Alexander Pope*, ed. Elwin–Courthope, viii. 79 (31 May 1724).
[3] 'Loeb' translation.
[4] Chalmers, xix. 256.                              [5] 'Loeb' translation.

Fenton does not dare to omit the incident altogether, but he tries his best to veil its indecency with an elaborate periphrasis:

> He said: and of the steer before him plac'd,
> That sinewy fragment at Ulysses cast,
> Where to the pastern-bone, by nerves combin'd,
> The well-horn'd foot indissolubly join'd.[1]

If the missile has not become even yet entirely heroic it is not the fault of the translator. He, at least, has wrapped it up in a napkin of poetic diction. To introduce humble and un-dignified facts into epic poetry was to Fenton like bringing pots and pans into the dining-room and setting them on the glossy sideboard with worthier and more polite vessels. The eighteenth-century poet believed in rendering unto Apollo the things he reckoned to be Apollo's; and whatever might be proper to the familiar epistle or the mock-heroic, the epic was held to demand from the poet a heightening of thought and expression well above the ordinary. In the same spirit eighteenth-century sculptors were accustomed to portraying contemporary English statesmen in the Roman toga. 'We go so far', Reynolds admits, 'as hardly to bear a statue in any other drapery.'[2] It is not, therefore, surprising to find him assuring his students that

the manner in which poetry is offered to the ear, the tone in which it is recited, should be as far removed from the tone of conversation, as the words of which that poetry is composed. . . . Whatever is familiar, or in any way reminds us of what we see and hear every day, perhaps does not belong to the higher provinces of art, either in poetry or painting.[3]

Pope was well aware that a translator must accept the sim-plicities of Homer, and not try to write him up where the original does not justify such treatment.

There is a real beauty [he saw] in an easy, pure, perspicuous de-scription, even of a low action. . . . Whenever the poet is obliged by the nature of his subject to descend to the lower manner of writing, an elevated style would be affected, and therefore ridiculous.[4]

But when it came to the pinch Pope seems to have become con-scious of the ladies and gentlemen who had subscribed (at a guinea a volume) for his translation, and he usually spares them

---

[1] Chalmers, xix. 258.          [2] *Discourses*, p. 123.
[3] Ibid., p. 215.
[4] Postscript to the *Odyssey*, Chalmers, xix. 278.

too sharp a contact with the actual. Broome, too, was equally circumspect. Where Homer had written:

Now so long as my men had grain and red wine they kept their hands from the cattle, for they were eager to save their lives. But when all the stores had been consumed from out the ship, they must needs roam about in search of game, fishes, and fowl, and whatever might come to their hands, fishing with bent hooks, for hunger pinched their bellies[1]—

Broome feels impelled to translate:

> Unhurt the beeves, untouch'd the woolly train
> Low through the grove, or range the flowery plain:
> Then fail'd our food; then fish we make our prey,
> Or fowl that screaming haunt the watery way.
> Till now, from sea or flood no succour found,
> Famine and meagre want besieg'd us round.[2]

Or again:

The mother sat at her hearth with her handmaidens, spinning the yarn of purple dye . . .[3]

becomes in Fenton:

> the Queen her hours bestow'd
> In curious works; the whirling spindle glow'd
> With crimson threads, while busy damsels cull
> The snowy fleece, or twist the purpled wool.[4]

The process here is not simply one of refining: Fenton has amplified, and he has also managed to impart a rhetorical excitement ('whirling', 'glowed', 'busy') which is perhaps endemic in the heroic couplet. In Homer's less emphatic hexameters it is no doubt easier to say simple things simply. Yet refinement is certainly responsible for many of the modifications made by Pope and his assistants.

It is the same when he tries his hand at modernizing Chaucer. When Chaucer has a thing to say he goes the shortest way about it; the thing felt or thought is expressed with the minimum of fuss. But Pope, for a variety of reasons—because 'old Chaucer' is too naïve, or too frank, or too unadorned—feels bound to give him a different turn. So we have Chaucer's

> And folwed ay his bodily delyt
> On wommen, there-as was his appetyt—

<hr>

[1] 'Loeb' translation (Book XII).  
[3] 'Loeb' translation (Book VI).  
[2] Chalmers, xix. 223.  
[4] Chalmers, xix. 193.

softened by Pope to

> Yet led astray by Venus' soft delights,
> He scarce cou'd rule some idle appetites;[1]

and Chaucer's

> Now wolde God that it were waxen night,
> And that the night wolde lasten evermo!

conventionalized to

> Restless he sate, invoking ev'ry pow'r
> To speed his bliss, and haste the happy hour.[2]

Pope is here turning Chaucer's natural (and therefore *perpetually* fresh) English into the fashionable idiom of a later century, the sort of idiom that softens the blow of actuality by referring to a birth in the family as 'a happy event'. We are not therefore surprised to find Pope in his ironical *Art of Sinking in Poetry* counselling the poet who wishes to excel in bathos to be sure to paint nature 'in her lowest simplicity' (ch. v), and to 'familiarize his mind to the lowest objects' (ch. vii). To this end, he adds, 'vulgar conversation will greatly contribute'.

As might be expected, the eighteenth-century reader had some difficulty in taking the old English and Scottish ballads seriously.[3] He was the victim of his own 'good taste'. If one has gone to the best masters in pianoforte it seems ridiculous to sit and listen to a penny whistle, and still more so to take it seriously. In his two interesting attempts to gain a hearing for the ballads of 'Chevy Chase' and 'The Two Children in the Wood', it is significant that Addison did not offer to defend the way in which they were expressed. In his discussion of the first he cautioned the reader not to let the simplicity of the style blind him to the greatness of the thought. In the second, he admitted that there is 'a despicable simplicity in the verse', and that the author has told his story 'in such an abject phrase and poorness of expression' that to quote him would only invite a laugh. But the thoughts are natural, 'and therefore cannot fail to please those who are not judges of language'.[4] Not knowing any better, he implies, they will not be disgusted by the familiarity and naked simplicity of the expression. Those who *are* judges of languages will inevitably (Addison supposes) be put

---

[1] *The Poems of Alexander Pope* ('Twickenham' edition), ed. G. Tillotson, ii. 16.
[2] Ibid. 32.   [3] See Note J, p. 170.
[4] *Spectator*, Nos. 70, 74; No. 85.

off by the humble expressions, but they should still be able to appreciate the natural thoughts, if they have 'a true and unprejudiced taste of nature'.

If Chaucer could be modernized, why not the ballads? If language is only 'the dress of thought' we can have a new dress whenever we want one, and the ballad—a sort of Cinderella among the literary Kinds—can come sparkling forth in a new gown and in the latest fashion. So, more than once, it did, and in so doing it completely lost its original character.

One of the most interesting examples of an eighteenth-century poet transmuting the work of an earlier day is Prior's treatment of 'The Nut-Brown Maid'. Prior had a genuine admiration for this old poem, or he would not have set to work upon it; he must have admired the natural feeling so simply and directly expressed. But in his 'Henry and Emma' this feeling has all but evaporated. What Prior has done is not so much to translate the poem into modern English as to inject it with some sort of poetical serum which completely alters the blood-content. He has treated it as a modern choreographer might treat some fairy-tale so as to evolve from it a delicate and sophisticated ballet. Emma, who undergoes a transformation similar to that of Liza in Shaw's *Pygmalion*, has become 'the dame' at whose feet Henry has often breathed his 'amorous vows'. Upon a spreading beech-tree

> Henry, in knots involving Emma's name,
> Had half express'd, and half conceal'd his flame.[1]

When, in the old poem, the Man asks the Maid if she could bear to marry an outlaw, a banished man—

Yet take good hede; for ever I drede that ye coude nat susteyne
The thornie wayes, the depe valeies, the snowe, the frost, the rayne,
The colde, the hete: for, drye or wete, we must lodge on the playne;
And us above, none other rofe, but a brake, bush, or twayne:
Which sone sholde greve you, I beleve, and ye wolde gladly than
That I had to the grene wode go, alone, a banyshed man—

Prior's Henry inquires:

> But canst thou, tender maid, canst thou sustain
> Afflictive want, or hunger's pressing pain?
> Those limbs, in lawn and softest silk array'd,
> From sunbeams guarded, and of winds afraid;

[1] Chalmers, x. 173.

Can they bear angry Jove? can they resist
The parching dog-star, and the bleak north-east?
When, chill'd by adverse snows and beating rain,
We tread with weary steps the longsome plain;
When with hard toil we seek our evening food,
Berries and acorns, from the neighbouring wood;
And find among the cliffs no other house,
But the thin covert of some gather'd boughs;
Wilt thou not then reluctant send thine eye
Around the dreary waste; and weeping try
(Though then, alas! that trial be too late)
To find thy father's hospitable gate,
And seats, where ease and plenty brooding sate?[1]

If it is asked whether the eighteenth-century lover talked to his
mistress like this, the answer is, No; nor did the Elizabethan
lover talk like Romeo. But in so far as Henry's language is the
language of gallantry it would be perfectly well understood by
the eighteenth-century fine lady, to whom it would also be,
in its own affected fashion, the language of the heart. To
Johnson, it is true, Prior's love poetry was in general 'unaffect-
ing or remote', and 'Henry and Emma' in particular 'a dull
and tedious dialogue'.[2] But Johnson's reactions were not always
typical of his century, and his poor opinion of Prior's love poetry
is partly accounted for by his inveterate distaste for the mytho-
logical trimmings of Venus, Cupid, and the rest which Prior
introduced so profusely into his work. To set against Johnson's
adverse criticism there is the testimony not only of Horace
Walpole (who was, of course, the sort of reader that Prior had
in mind) but also the poet Cowper, who can hardly be accused
of any want of natural feeling. 'There are few readers of poetry
of either sex in this country', Cowper wrote, 'who cannot remember how that entertaining piece has bewitched them.'[3]
There are not many of whom those words could be spoken to-
day. Indeed, 'Henry and Emma' is to eighteenth-century
poetry what 'The Idiot Boy' or 'Simon Lee' are to the poetry
of Wordsworth: a test which only the initiated are likely to pass.
To the open-minded reader, however, Prior's poem has still
some of the charm of a period piece, if nothing more.

[1] Ibid. 174 f.     [2] *Lives*, ii. 202 f.
[3] W. Cowper, *Life and Works*, ed. R. Southey, 1836–7, iv. 170 (Johnson, *Lives*,
ii. 203). The poem was also a favourite with Lady Mary Wortley Montagu. Even
in old age she could repeat it by heart.

Why so many people come with an open and receptive mind to eighteenth-century furniture, architecture, or music, and yet approach the poetry of that period with a closed and even hostile mind is something of a mystery. A Chippendale chair is a period piece and is willingly accepted as such; but when the reader of poetry comes upon some equally perfect period piece in the work of John Gay he is, as often as not, far less ready to respond to the fashion of an earlier age. The average reader of poetry, it may be, is not content with a purely aesthetic pleasure; he looks for some reflection, or at least adumbration, of his own habitual thoughts and feelings in the poem he happens to be reading. It is in the poetry of his own generation that he has most chance of finding it—or, if he is not quite abreast of his own day, in that of a generation back. If he does read the poetry of past ages he is apt to prefer what comes nearest in spirit to the poetry of his own day. If this is his habitual approach to poetry, then a good deal of the most characteristic work of the eighteenth-century poets will seem remote enough from his field of interest. But much of it—at its most remote, and even because of that remoteness—is capable of yielding a genuine aesthetic pleasure, the sort of pleasure that he may be accustomed to receiving from a Chelsea shepherdess or a conversation-piece by Zoffany. Gay at his best is among the most finished artists in that sophisticated and artificial style. He transmutes the raw materials of life into something at once delicate and artificial and remote. As with the chef in the *Dunciad*, working his culinary miracles,

> Beeves, at his touch, at once to jelly turn.

When Gay thinks of summer days in London he sees the lovers lying in the long grass beyond 'the dusty town', but before he has finished with them they have merged in his gentle mockery into the setting for a modern pastoral:

> When the sweet-breathing spring unfolds the buds,
> Love flys the dusty town for shady woods . . .
> Then Chelsea's meads o'erhear perfidious vows,
> And the prest grass defrauds the grazing cows.[1]

Perhaps no eighteenth-century poet got so much fun and so much beauty out of the poetic diction of the period as Gay. In *Rural Sports* and *Trivia* he revels in its absurdity, its dangerous

---

[1] 'An Epistle to the Right Honorable William Pulteney, Esq.', ll. 100 ff.

dignity, its exquisite artificiality, and its serenity. He takes it seriously—more so, for example, than Cowper—but not too seriously; he delights in it, he has a delicate understanding of its possibilities, and so he can produce *objets d'art* in verse, completely satisfying to the aesthetic sense, and with no more (but no less) importance than a vase from the workshops of Josiah Wedgewood.

II

If the twentieth-century reader is prepared to smile at Fenton's nervous approach to the cow-heel and the black puddings, he is not so ready to forgive another aspect of eighteenth-century refinement—the tacit assumption that the poor and the humble were not worth taking very seriously. It was an assumption that the novelists—from Defoe, Richardson, and Fielding onwards—were steadily undermining, but that the poets, for various reasons, were slower to discard. The normal attitude of the eighteenth-century poet to the peasant ought not to shock or surprise us; it does not differ noticeably from the attitude of the Oxford or Cambridge undergraduate of to-day to his scout or gyp, or of the average Londoner to a 'cabby', or of the normal housewife to her 'char'. In all but exceptional circumstances the usual relationship is still one of good-natured condescension to an inferior: a gentleman will take care that his condescension does not become too apparent, but when he is alone with his friends he will be quite undemocratically facetious about the cabby or the scout or the gyp. The twentieth-century novelist still considers himself entitled to make fun of butlers and taxi-drivers and charwomen; it has always been the most important literary function of the poor to provide comic relief. If you make fun of a cabinet minister that is satire; if you make fun of a taxi-driver or a country bumpkin it is comedy. But we no longer permit our poets to make that sort of fun. Since the days of Wordsworth it has become customary to assume that to any real poet not only the meanest flower that blows, but the humblest man that walks the earth, ought invariably to give 'thoughts that do often lie too deep for tears'. It is a remarkable tribute to Wordsworth that we should think so. To that great poet it seemed self-evident that pride,

> Howe'er disguised in its own majesty,
> Is littleness; that he who feels contempt

For any living thing, hath faculties
Which he has never used; that thought with him
Is in its infancy.[1]

There was little of this feeling in the eighteenth century, and the poets did not do much to encourage its growth. What, for instance, are we to make of Lady Mary Wortley Montagu? When Pope, still troubled by the sudden death of John Hewet and Sarah Drew, told her all about it in his letter and enclosed the epitaph he had written, Lady Mary (who was on her way home from Paris) replied in a letter so devastatingly facetious that we can scarcely read it to-day without a feeling of discomfort.

I must applaud your good-nature [she tells Pope] in supposing that your pastoral lovers (vulgarly called haymakers) would have lived in everlasting joy and harmony if the lightning had not interrupted their scheme of happiness. . . . Since you desire me to try my skill in an epitaph, I think the following lines perhaps more just, though not so poetical as yours:

> Here lie John Hughes and Sarah Drew;
> Perhaps you'll say, what's that to you?
> Believe me, friend, much may be said
> On this poor couple that are dead.
> On Sunday next they should have married;
> But see how oddly things are carried!
> On Thursday last it rained and lighten'd;
> These tender lovers, sadly frighten'd,
> Shelter'd beneath the cocking hay,
> In hopes to pass the storm away;
> But the bold thunder found them out
> (Commission'd for that end, no doubt),
> And, seizing on their trembling breath,
> Consign'd them to the shades of death.
> Who knows if 'twas not kindly done?
> For had they seen the next year's sun,
> A beaten wife and cuckold swain
> Had jointly curs'd the marriage chain;
> Now they are happy in their doom,
> For P. has wrote upon their tomb.

I confess these sentiments are not altogether so heroic as yours; but I hope you will forgive them in favour of the two last lines. . . .[2]

---

[1] 'Lines left upon a Seat in a Yew-tree', 1795, ll. 50 ff.
[2] *The Works of Alexander Pope*, ed. Elwin–Courthope, ix. 409 f.

Perhaps if Lady Mary, and not Pope, had been staying at
Stanton Harcourt when the storm broke she might have felt
differently about John Hewet (not Hughes, as she has it)
and Sarah Drew. Something, too, should be allowed for the
fact that most of us tend to resist a direct call upon our sympathy, though we may respond readily enough if we are not so
prompted. But Lady Mary's reaction to Pope's rural tragedy
is quite clear: she thinks that he is making altogether too much
fuss over a couple of mere villagers. These are people that one
would scarcely notice at all if they were alive: why grow heroic
about them merely because they have come to a sudden end?
If the bolt had struck Lord Harcourt, that *would* have been
something! Her response does at least indicate how such an
incident was apt to strike an aristocratic lady in the eighteenth
century. Pope had asked her to take his rustic lovers seriously;
but his epitaph was not nearly good enough to persuade her
to alter her habitual attitude to such folk.

What prevented the average eighteenth-century poet from being
fully conscious of his common humanity with the poor was not so
much an economic inequality as an inequality in education. He
talked a different language from the poor man, he had a wider
range of ideas and interests. For a century in which polite expression meant so much, the barrier erected between the classes by
a different mode of speech was almost insuperable. The full
significance of Wordsworth's heresy about adopting or adapting
the language of humble and rustic life for poetry will not be
apparent unless we can realize what such a suggestion would
have meant to Lady Mary Wortley Montagu or Lord Chesterfield, or even to a man of such comprehensive sympathies as
Edmund Burke. The normal attitude to the poor in the
eighteenth century was, as has been suggested, one of good-
natured condescension to Goody Smith or Gaffer Brown or
Granny White. So Goldsmith, the kindly but amused spectator
from a different *monde*, recalls the village inn, where the country
innocents were to be seen relaxing in characteristic attitudes—

> Where grey-beard mirth, and smiling toil retired,
> Where village statesmen talked with looks profound,
> And news much older than their ale went round.[1]

No one would question the kindliness of that, but the rustics are

[1] *The Deserted Village*, ll. 222 ff.

not Simon Lees or Betty Foys; they are much nearer to being the fauna of the place—only a little more important to Goldsmith than the flora, or the noisy geese that gabbled o'er the pool, or the varnished clock that clicked behind the door. Goldsmith makes more of his rustics than most eighteenth-century poets, but he remains aware of their limitations as poetic material. Those limitations were set forth by Johnson with all his customary candour:

The state of a man confined to the employments and pleasures of the country, is so little diversified, and exposed to so few of those accidents which produce perplexities, terrors, and surprises, in more complicated transactions, that he can be shown but seldom in such circumstances as attract curiosity. His ambition is without policy, and his love without intrigue. He has no complaints to make of his rival, but that he is richer than himself; nor any disasters to lament, but a cruel mistress or a bad harvest.[1]

All of which, Johnson suggests, makes for dull poetry, since a man only becomes interesting when he has arrived at a stage of some emotional and intellectual complexity. In direct opposition to this statement of Johnson's may be placed the equally downright assertion of Wordsworth about humble and rustic people. 'From their rank of society and the sameness and narrow circle of their intercourse'—they are not just dull or boring with the tedious repetition of their unsophisticated notions, but—'being less under the influence of social vanity, they convey their feelings and notions in simple and unelaborated expressions.'[2] And what they have to convey—'the essential passions of the heart'—is what interests Wordsworth, as man and poet. Johnson and Wordsworth, it will be noticed, start from precisely the same premiss (that rustic life is simple, unvaried, and narrow in scope), and arrive at exactly the opposite conclusions. It is not that Johnson did not know a good deal about the essential passions of the heart; it is certainly not that he lacked any feeling of common humanity with the poor. He had known poverty, and he never ceased to know the poor. It is therefore all the more significant that it is Johnson—and not Lord Chesterfield or Horace Walpole—who undertakes to demonstrate that the rustic poor have only a limited value for poetry. They failed to interest the eighteenth

---

[1] *Rambler*, No. 36, 21 July 1750.
[2] *Wordsworth's Literary Criticism*, p. 14.

century deeply in the same way, and for much the same reason, as children failed to interest Pope or Gray: they were not fully adult, they were intellectually immature, and their sentiments and expressions were crude. The century's normal attitude here was that expressed by Hume in his essay on 'Refinement in Writing':

Sentiments which are merely natural affect not the mind with any pleasure, and seem not worthy of our attention. The pleasantries of a waterman, the observations of a peasant, the ribaldry of a porter or hackney coachman, all of these are natural, and disagreeable. . . . Nothing can please persons of taste, but nature drawn with all her graces and ornaments, *la belle nature*; or if we copy low life, the strokes must be strong and remarkable, and must convey a lively image to the mind.[1]

It follows therefore that if pastoral poetry is to be made tolerable to a polite age the poet must shun any strict adherence to the sort of life actually led by shepherds, since (as Johnson observed) 'according to the customs of modern life, it is improbable that shepherds should be capable of harmonious numbers, or delicate sentiments'[2]—and both were required by the eighteenth-century reader. Shepherds are accordingly to be described 'as they may be conceived then to have been, when the best of men followed the employment'.[3] What to an eighteenth-century poet was the logical outcome of describing country folk 'as at this day they really are' Gay showed in *The Shepherd's Week*, and Pope demonstrated even more hilariously in the mock ballad of Roger and Cicely which he inserted in his *Guardian* essay on Philips's *Pastorals*:

But the most beautiful example of this kind that I ever met with, is in a very valuable piece, which I chanced to find among some old manuscripts, entituled, *A Pastoral Ballad*: which I think, for its nature and simplicity, may (notwithstanding the modesty of the title) be allowed a perfect pastoral: It is composed in the *Somersetshire* dialect, and the names such as are proper to the country people. It may be observed, as a further beauty of this pastoral, the words *Nymph, Dryad, Naiad, Fawn, Cupid*, or *Satyr*, are not once mentioned through the whole. I shall make no apology for inserting some few lines of

---

[1] David Hume, *Essays Moral, Political and Literary*, ed. T. H. Green and T. H. Grose, 1912, i. 240.
[2] *Rambler*, No. 37, 24 July 1750.
[3] 'A Discourse on Pastoral Poetry', prefixed to Pope's *Pastorals*.

this excellent piece. *Cicely* breaks thus into the subject, as she is
going a-milking:

*Cicely*.   Rager go vetch tha kee, or else tha zun
        Will quite be go, be vore c' have half a don.
*Roger*.   Thou shouldst not ax ma tweece, but I've a be
        To dreave our bull to bull tha parson's kee.

And so forth, ending with the lines:

> So Rager parted vor to vetch tha kee,
> And vor her bucket in went Cicely.[1]

That, then, is Pope's *reductio ad absurdum* of Ambrose Philips's
*simplesse*. John Hewet and Sarah Drew might qualify for an
epitaph, but Pope would see to it that they never strayed into
pastoral poetry.

As the century wore on, this attitude to the poor began very
gradually to change. In his *Elegy* Gray is reminding his readers
that the great and the important must die like everyone else;
death is not a fate reserved only for the poor and humble.
*Some* of the humble folk, it is true, might in more affluent circumstances have become famous, but 'their lot forbad'. Never
mind: it also forbade them to grow great in wickedness. The
poor, then, are taken seriously in the *Elegy*; but it is rather the
deadness of the dead, and the universality of death (made all the
more apparent by the anonymity of the mouldering heaps distinguished by no 'storied urn or animated bust'), that the poet's
imagination has seized most firmly. As a man of culture Gray
still has a decent respect for the storied urn, and is even prepared to be slightly apologetic about the frail memorials of the
villagers, with 'their uncouth rhymes and shapeless sculpture
deck'd'—the lapidary equivalent of ballads and broadsides in
literature. He is still, in fact, thinking of 'the rude forefathers
of the hamlet'. Goldsmith is perhaps more democratic, a
humorous soul who was probably quite as much at ease with his
landlady as with Burke or Johnson; but Goldsmith, too, with
his smith who 'relaxes his pond'rous strength and leans to hear',
or his swain 'mistrustless of his smutted face', or his awed rustics
listening to the polysyllabic disputation of parson and schoolmaster, is hardly taking his rustics quite seriously. You do not
feel that anyone in the village is quite adult. Cowper, too, is
still (for all his sympathy and interest) one of the gentlefolk

---

[1] *Guardian*, No. 40, 27 Apr. 1713.

writing naturally of 'swains' and 'boors' and of the woodman with 'the short tube that fumes beneath his nose'.

The change comes, when it does come, not so much in the habitual way of seeing the poor as a different race (for that continues) as in a greater readiness to feel for them *when they are in distress*. This may be seen, as early as 1730, in some lines of James Thomson:

> Ah! little think the gay licentious proud,
> Whom pleasure, power, and affluence surround—
> They, who their thoughtless hours in giddy mirth,
> And wanton, often cruel, riot waste—
> Ah! little think they, while they dance along,
> How many feel, this very moment, death
> And all the sad variety of pain; . . .
> How many pine in want, and dungeon-glooms; . . .
>     . . . sore pierced by wintry winds,
> How many sink into the sordid hut
> Of cheerless poverty. . . .[1]

If men would only think of these things, and of the 'incessant struggle' that life means for so many unfortunate wretches,

> The social tear would rise, the social sigh;
> And into clear perfection, gradual bliss,
> Refining still, the social passions work.

In the same way Goldsmith's voice changes when he pictures to himself 'yon widow'd, solitary thing', the last survivor of the now depopulated village,

>       forced in age, for bread,
> To strip the brook with mantling cresses spread,
> To pick her wintry faggot from the thorn,
> To seek her nightly shed, and weep till morn. . . .[2]

Cowper, too, has his Crazy Kate in *The Task*.[3]

Such miseries and such destitution made Goldsmith and Cowper sad; it is not until we come to Crabbe that we find a poet whom they make positively angry. The anger may not lead to better poetry, but it does suggest that the point of view has altered. Yet even Crabbe is still for the most part the *spectator ab extra*, moved by the hard lot of the poorer classes, and distressed by their shiftlessness and improvidence, but not

---

[1] *The Seasons*, 'Winter', ll. 322 ff.      [2] *The Deserted Village*, ll. 130 ff.
[3] Op. cit. i. 534 ff.

particularly interested in their minds. For that sort of interest (if we except Burns, who was one of them) we have to wait till Wordsworth. We never really get it in Coleridge, Byron, Shelley, or Keats. It was Wordsworth, almost alone among the Romantic poets, who

> saw into the depth of human souls,
> Souls that appear to have no depth at all
> To careless eyes.[1]

But it is a common mistake to assume that we are all Wordsworths now, and that the common human attitude to the poor (as distinct from the provision made for them) has radically, altered since the days of Pope and Swift. We are all Wordsworths now only when Wordsworth has shown us the way. Left to ourselves, most of us still approach a tramp or a charwoman with meagre expectations, and with a conscious or unconscious adjustment of our mental attitude.

[1] *The Prelude*, xiii. 166 ff.

# VI
## SOME LIMITATIONS

### I

A SOCIETY which assumes that a correct taste in poetry is one of the natural rewards for being a lady or a gentleman will almost inevitably have to be given its poetry in a diluted form. Where all, or nearly all, are to enjoy the entertainment provided, the poet must make himself intelligible, if not to the meanest capacities, then at least to all but the most stubbornly prosaic. If the men of wit and taste (for whom Swift claimed that he had written *A Tale of a Tub*) were to be the readers and judges of poetry, the poet must write so as to be not only intelligible, but *immediately* intelligible. Men of wit and taste have so much to do, so many books to read or to turn over, so many visits to pay—to the Opera, the concert of vocal and orchestral music, the exhibition of new paintings, the ridotto, the rout at my Lady Mary's, Signior Lunardi's ascent in his balloon— that they cannot be expected to wrestle with obscurities or dig for hidden meanings that are not already sparkling on the surface for all to see. Nothing less than this immediate intelligibility was demanded by Thomas Tickell in 1711. Obscurity, he insists, is

of all qualities the most incongruous with the nature of poetry, since, unless poetry is taken in at the first glance, it immediately loses its force and point.[1]

It may be doubted whether many reputable critics of the period would have demanded so much—or so little—of poetry; but if Tickell goes too far, he is only giving unusual emphasis to a belief which was widely current at the time. As early as 1679 Dryden is grumbling that Shakespeare's style is 'so pestered with figurative expressions, that it is as affected as it is obscure'.[2] Dryden's complaint has at least this justification that it is made against a writer whose speeches have to be heard and understood in a theatre, but, in fact, he would have been willing to

---

[1] From 'De Poesi Didactica', an unpublished lecture delivered in 1711 (R. E. Tickell, *Thomas Tickell and the Eighteenth Century Poets*, 1931, p. 203; quoted by F. W. Bateson, *English Poetry and the English Language*, 1934, p. 52). See Note K, p. 170.
[2] *Essays*, i. 203.

extend his criticism to non-dramatic poetry too. The popularity
of Spenser in the eighteenth century is almost certainly due in
some measure to his perfect lucidity, his unfailing harmony of
thought and expression: the popularity of Shakespeare was
achieved in spite of the obscurity of his language, which Dryden
and others were constantly diluting in their adaptations.

The ridicule of Gray's Pindaric Odes in the 1750s and of
Christopher Smart's *Song to David* in the 1760s was based on
the same assumption, that all poetry ought to be intelligible (in
much the same way as prose is intelligible) to the ordinary cultivated reader. David Garrick offered some consolation to Gray
for the reception of his Odes by the contemporary public:

> Repine not, Gray, that our weak dazzled eyes
>   Thy daring heights and brightness shun;
> How few can track the eagle to the skies,
>   Or like him gaze upon the sun.
>
> The gentle reader loves the gentle Muse,
>   That little dares, and little means,
> Who humbly sips her learning from *Reviews*,
>   Or flutters in the *Magazines*.[1]

But long before Garrick's day Dryden had settled his account
with the Dick Minims of his own generation:

Are all the flights of Heroic Poetry to be concluded bombast,
unnatural, and mere madness, because they are not affected with
their excellencies? It is just as reasonable to conclude there is no day,
because a blind man cannot distinguish of light and colours. Ought
they not rather, in modesty, to doubt of their own judgments, when
they think this or that expression in Homer, Virgil, Tasso, or Milton's
*Paradise*, to be too far strained, than positively to conclude that 'tis
all fustian, and mere nonsense? 'Tis true, there are limits to be set
betwixt the boldness and rashness of a poet; but he must understand
those limits who pretends to judge as well as he who undertakes to
write. . . .[2]

Much the same retort was made by James Thomson in 1726:

The truth of the case is this: These weak-sighted gentlemen cannot bear the strong light of poetry and the finer and more amusing[3]
scene of things it displays. But must those therefore whom heaven
has blessed with the discerning eye shut it to keep them company?[4]

---

[1] *The Oxford Book of Eighteenth Century Verse*, ed. D. Nichol Smith, p. 408.
[2] *Essays*, i. 182.   [3] i.e. engaging the mind or attention in a pleasing way;
interesting. (*O.S.D.*).   [4] Preface to the second edition of 'Winter', 1726.

But in 1726 the men of wit and taste were still confident that there was nothing wrong with their poetical sight or their own competence to discriminate. Why indeed should they doubt their own judgements, when they expected the same measure of lucidity from poetry as they found in a *Tatler* or *Spectator* essay, and usually got it?

Eighteenth-century poetic theory and practice, in fact, were based on a consideration for the reader which must seem to the twentieth century (accustomed to taking many hard knocks from its poets) almost unaccountable. The poet was a member of polite society addressing himself to his equals, and though poetry was a special mode of communication it did not exempt him from all the normal usages of polite society. If you invited him to make one at a dinner-party, you expected him to talk intelligibly; if he published a volume of poems you expected him to write the sort of thing that the average well-educated man could understand because it came within the orbit of his own experience. If he had (as we all have) some purely private thoughts and feelings and relationships and experiences, you expected him to keep those to himself, and not embarrass your dinner-party with them, or even bring them into his poems.

How far a compact and well-organized reading public, unusually confident in its own powers of judgement, compelled the poet to remain at the level of the least imaginative—how far Dryden's (or Pope's or Gray's) car was 'less presumptuous' because the public would have it so—it would be hard to tell. Yet the very demand for poetry in the eighteenth century undoubtedly had an adverse effect on the quality of what was supplied; for the poet, aware that he had a very fair chance of being widely read, took perhaps too much care to be easily readable. No doubt, too, there is a necessary connexion between what oft was thought and what can be immediately understood, and Wordsworth for one appears to have noticed it. In the *Prelude* he glances with contempt at those writers (and he is obviously thinking of his own immediate predecessors in English poetry) who

> Effeminately level down the truth
> To certain general notions, for the sake
> Of being understood at once. . . .[1]

[1] Op. cit. xiii. 212 ff.

H

This is perhaps the most damaging criticism of eighteenth-century poetry that Wordsworth ever uttered. The very qualities that made it available for a wide reading public limited at the same time its intrinsic value.

## II

It has already been suggested that the emphasis which polite society places on good taste had a restrictive effect on the range of eighteenth-century poetry.[1] There is no reason why good taste should not be positive and active, the expression of a man's liking for this or his admiration of that. In practice, however, it tends to express itself in a fastidious shrinking from, or even rejection of, all such experience as passes beyond a moderate intensity. It avoids the disturbing, the unusual, and asserts itself by condemning whatever it has difficulty in assimilating. So we find Lord Chesterfield endlessly deploring the too emphatic, or recoiling from natural pleasures in the name of good taste. More surprisingly, we find Shenstone seriously pondering the deleterious effect of Spenser on a cultivated taste:

One may entertain some doubt whether the perusal of his monstrous descriptions be not as prejudicial to true taste, as it is advantageous to the extent of imagination. Spenser to be sure expands the last, but then he expands it beyond its due limits. After all, there are many favorite passages in his Fairy Queen, which will be instances of a great and cultivated genius misapplied.[2]

Here the gap between the eighteenth and the twentieth centuries is at its widest. Few readers of poetry to-day would admit that the imagination had any 'due limits' at all; and if it came to a conflict between imagination and 'true taste' it would be true taste that gave way. But the eighteenth-century poet, so conscious of his public, so sharply aware of the men of wit and taste who were to read and judge his poetry, was compelled at times to call in his wandering thoughts and suppress his wayward fancies. Writing to Mrs. Thrale about some stanzas he had written on Sir John Lade's coming of age, Johnson remarks:

I have enclosed a short song of congratulation, which you must not shew to any body. It is odd that it should come into any bodies head.[3]

The verses a poet showed only to his friends were sometimes

---

[1] See above, p. 84.   [2] *Works*, ed. cit. ii. 186.
[3] *The Poems of Samuel Johnson*, ed. David Nichol Smith and Edward L. McAdam, 1941, p. 195.

a good deal more imaginative and reckless than those he
made public. One of the freshest and most natural voices in
eighteenth-century poetry is that of Matthew Green. He wrote
*The Spleen* with no thought of publication, and it was not, in
fact, published until after his death. It was written for his own
amusement and for the pleasure of the friend to whom it was
addressed; and Green, who did not regard himself as a professional poet, felt free to think and write as he pleased. He pays
the Muses 'only transient visits', he says,

> Scarce known to the fastidious dames,
> Nor skill'd to call them by their names . . . .
> On poems by their dictates writ,
> Critics, as sworn appraisers, sit,
> And mere upholst'rers in a trice
> On gems and paintings set a price.
> These tayl'ring artists for our lays
> Invent cramp'd rules, and with straight stays
> Striving free Nature's shape to hit,
> Emaciate sense, before they fit.[1]

Unembarrassed by the rules, unhampered by good taste or even
by any consciousness of being in public, Green takes little risks
with his own mind with varying degrees of success ('news, the
manna of the day'; movements 'tarantulated by a tune';
morning 'smear'd by th' embraces of the night'; 'the ear-
lechery of men'; politicians 'grazing on ether in the Park'; the
'soft violence of pray'r'; 'the feather'd throng, Who pay their
quit-rents with a song'; 'av'rice, sphincter of the heart' . . .). It
is clear that Green had an original turn of mind: what is significant is that he did not discourage it. One of the very few
anecdotes about Green concerns his conversation; it was as
unorthodox as his poetry, 'which occasioned one of the com-
missioners of the Customs, a very dull man, to observe that he
did not know how it was, but Green always expressed himself
in a different manner from other people'.[2] How many Matthew
Greens dwindled into orthodoxy in the eighteenth century we
can never know, but in that age it was far from easy to swim
against the stream. It was an age too that laid a dispropor-
tionate emphasis on good sense. The contemporary poet's
dilemma was perfectly expressed by St. Evremond:

Poetry requires a peculiar genius, that agrees not overmuch with

---

[1] Chalmers, xv. 167.          [2] Ibid., xv. 158.

good sense. It is sometimes the language of gods, sometimes of buffoons; rarely that of a gentleman.[1]

It was a dilemma almost peculiar to the eighteenth century.

### III

Quite apart from the effect that the reading public, by their expressed dissatisfaction or by the silent pressure of their mediocrity or their good taste, may have had on the mind of the poets, there was another contemporary tendency that helped to limit the range and complexity of eighteenth-century poetry. The mind of the age had set strongly in the direction of Simplicity—that Simplicity (as Swift put it) 'without which no human performance can arrive to any great perfection'.[2] The cult of simplicity is, of course, one expression of the neo-classical admiration for order and unity of design. The current objection to Gothic architecture was based, theoretically at least, on the assumption that the total effect was destroyed by a surfeit of detail. In surveying a Gothic building, Hume explained, the eye 'is disturbed by the multiplicity of ornaments, and loses the whole by its minute attention to the parts'.[3] Addison, in *Spectator*, No. 417, had expressed the normal taste of the Queen Anne men when he contrasted the 'mean' effect made by the interior of a Gothic cathedral with the 'great and amazing' impression made by the Pantheon at Rome. 'Lo, what huge heaps of littleness around!' Pope had written of Timon's elaborate villa; and Gray, gazing on the architectural complexities of Versailles, echoed him with 'What a huge heap of littleness!'[4] The eye of the beholder had grown accustomed to receiving a simple unified impression. Even the full-bottomed wig worn by Addison and his contemporaries has this simplifying and uniform effect; it reduces and formalizes the infinite variety of human faces to a familiar and almost architectural regularity.

In the poetry of the period we find this same simplifying process constantly at work. The poet aims at achieving the sort of unified impression that he was himself accustomed to receiving from contemporary architecture. Pope, indeed, makes

[1] *The Works of Monsieur De St. Evremond, Made English* .... The Second Edition, 1728, ii. 60.
[2] *Prose Works*, ed. Temple Scott, iii. 204.
[3] *Essays, Moral, Political and Literary*, ed. cit. i. 241.    [4] *Correspondence*, i. 107.

this obvious comparison when he is emphasizing the need to subordinate all the parts in a literary composition to the total effect:

> Thus when we view some well-proportion'd dome,
> (The *world's* just wonder, and ev'n *thine*, O Rome!)
> No single parts unequally surprize;
> All comes *united* to th' admiring eyes;
> No monstrous height, or breadth, or length appear;
> The *whole* at once is *bold*, and *regular*.[1]

One of the main quarrels of the eighteenth-century poet with the Metaphysicals was just that they failed to attain to this grand simplicity, and constantly clouded their meaning by leaving their thoughts only half-developed, or by starting more thoughts than the reader could comfortably absorb.

In them [Steele complains] one point of wit flashes so fast upon another, that the reader's attention is dazzled by the continual sparkling of their imagination; you find a new design started almost in every line, and you come to the end without the satisfaction of seeing any one of them executed.[2]

Here, once again, we have one of those differences of taste which make one age impatient with the art of another. The pendulum has at present swung back to the Metaphysicals. Complexity is to-day your only wear; and many (perhaps most) contemporary critics would be quite happy to adapt Swift's dictum to read: 'That complexity without which no poetical performance can arrive to any great perfection.' So far the twentieth century has shown less consistency in its taste than the eighteenth: if complexity has to-day become almost the supreme test for great poetry, the tendency has been rather in the opposite direction in some of the other arts, such as architecture, furniture, household fabrics. None the less, literature (and one must add literary criticism) are moving steadily farther away from that simplicity which Swift and Pope and their friends all admired; and we are now in danger of finding only insipidity and flatness where they found grandeur and strength, or else (refusing to believe the worst of them) discovering complexity where none exists.

An age which demands simplicity, unity of design, proportion, and symmetry from its artists, and which is uneasy unless it can comprehend quickly and without undue effort the effect of the

---

[1] *Essay on Criticism*, ll. 248 ff.      [2] *Guardian*, No. 16, 30 Mar. 1713.

whole, may be asking a good deal of those artists. It is also restricting them in the choice and treatment of their material. For an uncompromising statement of the issues involved we may turn to Shaftesbury:

It is an infallible proof of the want of just integrity in every writing, from the epopee or heroic poem down to the familiar epistle, or slightest essay either in verse or prose, if every several part or portion fits not its proper place so exactly, that the least transposition would be impracticable. . . . If there be any passage in the middle or end which might have stood in the beginning, or any in the beginning which might have stood as well in the middle or end; there is properly in such a piece neither beginning, middle, or end. It is a mere *rhapsody*, not a work.[1]

This is the sort of statement that very few Englishmen can be brought to take seriously. If it were to be applied to the national drama or the novel the results would be disastrous; and those plays and novels that passed the test, or came nearest to passing it, would not necessarily be among the greatest. The modern reader would be more likely to agree with Shaftesbury if he had merely claimed that nothing could be removed from a true work of art without loss. But Shaftesbury is obviously thinking of a literary structure much more compact and shapely than, say, Donne's *Second Anniversarie*, which to him would have seemed more a mental journey than a poem. He writes of poetry almost as he would write of architecture: a thought out of place or a thought too many is like a badly placed window, or a superfluous column in the Parthenon.

It should be said at once that such aesthetic severity was the ideal of poetry planners rather than the practice of the poets. The *Epistle to Dr. Arbuthnot* would not pass such rigorous tests, nor would much else written in the eighteenth century. But the unified effect, the shapely structure, the artistic whole arranged on bold and simple lines, did remain an ideal all through the period, and must inevitably have prompted the poets to deal only with such material as could be easily treated *in that way*. What was too subtle, or too complex, or what involved too difficult a reconciliation of opposites,[2] they left alone. They played for safety, they launched not beyond their depth; and only perhaps in the eighteenth century was discretion looked upon as one of the major virtues in an English poet.

[1] *Characteristics*, iii. 180 n.                    [2] See below, p. 155.

# VII
# NATURE

IT is relatively easy to detect the assumptions made by earlier
generations about the nature and purpose of poetry, and to
see that they were no more than assumptions; it is much more
difficult to realize that the twentieth century has formed or
inherited certain assumptions of its own, and that its attitude
to the poetry of past ages is unconsciously guided by those.
From the time of Wordsworth it has been commonly assumed
that Nature (trees, flowers, birds, mountains, and so on) must
necessarily form the subject of a large part—perhaps even the
chief part—of all poetry. 'There are two great subjects of
poetry', a critic tells us. 'One of these [is] the natural world. . . .
The other . . . is human nature.'[1] The sociable eighteenth
century gave to Nature a less prominent place, and held that
the proper study of mankind was not the river Duddon or the
Westmorland mountains, but Man. Natural description in
Pope is usually incidental, serving characteristically to adorn
or emphasize some statement or event, as it does, too, in the epic
similes of Homer and Virgil.

The eighteenth-century attitude to Nature is put clearly by
James Beattie. Human nature must always come first: *that*
never fails to arouse interest.

Human affairs and human feelings are universally interesting.
There are many who have no great relish for the poetry that deli-
neates only irrational or inanimate beings; but to that which exhi-
bits the fortunes, the characters, and the conduct of men, there is
hardly any person who does not listen with sympathy and delight. . . .
Mere descriptions, however beautiful, and moral reflections, however just, become tiresome where our passions are not occasionally
awakened by some event that concerns our fellow-men.[2]

When Beattie wrote these words he had not forgotten Thomson's *Seasons* and the many other descriptive poems such as
Mallet's *Excursion* and Savage's *Wanderer*. The descriptive poem
had become so familiar to readers of English poetry that in
1762 it was actually included among the recognized Kinds in a

---

[1] Stopford Brooke, *Naturalism in English Poetry*, 1920, p. 19.
[2] James Beattie, *Essays on Poetry and Music . . .*, 1776, p. 373. See Note L, p. 170.

well-known manual on poetry.[1] But to Beattie, as to most
eighteenth-century readers, Nature was always more interesting
when it was involved with Man.

Do not all readers of taste receive peculiar pleasure from those
little tales or episodes, with which Thomson's descriptive poem on
the Seasons is here and there enlivened? and are they not sensible,
that the thunderstorm would not have been half so interesting without the tale of the two lovers; nor the harvest-scene, without that of
Palemon and Lavinia; nor the driving snows, without the exquisite
picture of a man perishing among them?[2]

It was Man, walking amid the glad (or sad) creation, that
gave to Nature its crowning interest and justified the extended
description.

The taste for mountains and cataracts, for tempests and
floods, for the turbulence of stormy seas and the tortured and
fractured surfaces of the earth, has rightly been associated with
romanticism. The *normal* eighteenth-century preference was for
the natural scene that showed welcome signs of Man's occupa-
tion, for the cultivated landscape with smoke rising from
cottage chimneys, and the spire of the decent church topping
the neighbouring hill.[3] It was on such scenes that Cowper
looked out with quiet pleasure in the depths of his eighteenth-
century Buckinghamshire:

> . . . The distant plough slow-moving, and beside
> His labouring team that swerved not from the track,
> The sturdy swain diminished to a boy!
> Here Ouse, slow-winding through a level plain
> Of spacious meads with cattle sprinkled o'er,
> Conducts the eye along his sinuous course
> Delighted. There, fast rooted in their bank,
> Stand, never overlooked, our favourite elms,
> That screen the herdsman's solitary hut;
> While far beyond, and overthwart the stream,
> That, as with molten glass, inlays the vale,

[1] *The Art of Poetry on a New Plan*, 2 vols., 1762.

[2] *Essays on Poetry and Music* . . ., p. 374. Cf. Wordsworth, 'Essay Supplementary
to the Preface': 'In any well-used copy of the *Seasons* the book generally opens of
itself with the rhapsody on love, or with one of the stories (perhaps "Damon and
Musidora"); these also are prominent in our collections of Extracts, and are the
parts of his Work which, after all, were probably most efficient in first recommending the author to general notice.' (*Wordsworth's Literary Criticism*, p. 186 f.)

[3] The 'decent' church: decent because appropriate to its surroundings, customary, unostentatious, assuming its due and proper place in the landscape and in
the life of the community.

The sloping land recedes into the clouds;
Displaying, on its varied side, the grace
Of hedge-row beauties numberless, square tower,
Tall spire, from which the sound of cheerful bells
Just undulates upon the listening ear,
Groves, heaths, and smoking villages, remote.[1]

Yet such is the prestige of the great Romantic poets of the early nineteenth century that many readers still privately measure the intensity of a poet's experience by his preference for romantic landscapes rather than the more pastoral scenes which the eighteenth-century poet usually favoured. Is there some special virtue in waterfalls and precipices? Does the natural prospect please in proportion as it is emptied of all traces of Man? Or is Man to be admitted only as he is a solitary, a wanderer, an outcast from society? Apparently that good (and in some respects typical) eighteenth-century poet, James Thomson, was not far from thinking so. In the Preface to his 'Winter' he claims that

the best, both ancient and modern, poets have been passionately fond of retirement, and solitude. The wild romantic country was their delight. And they seem never to have been more happy, than when, lost in unfrequented fields, far from the little busy world, they were at leisure, to meditate, and sing the works of Nature.

Thomson supports this uncompromising statement by only two references, to the Book of Job and Virgil's *Georgics*. But here he was surely generalizing rashly: a preference for 'the wild romantic country' was genuine enough in Thomson himself, but it is as noticeably absent in other poets, such as Chaucer, or, among men of his own century, Cowper and Crabbe. A great deal of unnecessary controversy would be avoided if poets would only say, 'What I like in poetry is this, or that,' instead of saying categorically, 'Poetry is this' or 'The best poets always do that'. The love of romantic scenery forms an interesting chapter in the history of Taste, but half-way through the twentieth century we ought to be able to see this particular shift in human consciousness in its proper perspective. Precipices and cataracts may be more dramatic *per se* than a field of buttercups or ducks dabbling in a village pond, but they are not more 'poetical'.

More generally, the cult of Nature (and not merely Nature

[1] *The Task*, i. 160 ff.

as it appears in 'the wild romantic country') is due in large
measure to conditions of which the nineteenth and twentieth
centuries have little reason to be proud—the hideousness of our
towns and the triviality of urban life. When the contemporaries
of Pope thought of Nature they did not necessarily see it as a
blessed escape from the ugliness and the distracting roar and
bustle of the town. Their towns were, generally speaking, not
ugly, and for the upper classes the life lived in them had a
formal gaiety and variety that have now largely disappeared. In
such small cities as Norwich and Bristol there were bad slums,
and there were shocking slums in London; but there were also
wide areas of pleasant streets, dignified terraces, and spacious
squares. Critics sometimes write as if the men and women of
the early eighteenth century had no interest in the country-side
at all. 'When Pope was writing', we are told, 'the love of Nature
for itself had quite decayed.'[1] But this is wildly wrong. The
Restoration affectation that all beyond Hyde Park was a desert
had soon passed, though country cousins continued to be
laughed at, very naturally, in contemporary comedy. Pope,
the poet of the Town, passed most of his life, from choice, in the
country; in the summer, when the roads were dry, he frequently
rode off into the country on visits to his noble friends. Addison,
to whom the coffee-house was a second home, purchased a
small estate at Bilton in Warwickshire and took a great deal of
interest in its improvement. Nicholas Rowe had a cottage in
the country to which he frequently retired. Even Gay, the
most sedentary and urban of them all, spent considerable
periods with the Duke and Duchess of Queensberry in Wiltshire.
All this is either not known or too often forgotten; what is
remembered is Johnson's lack of enthusiasm for country life, or
Gibbon closeted in his library.

Having no prejudice (as the nineteenth century had) against
the artificial—delighting, in fact, in the products of art—the
eighteenth-century poet not unexpectedly tended to prefer
those scenes and those aspects of Nature which recalled to his
mind most pleasingly the works of Man. 'We find the works
of Nature', Addison told his readers, 'still more pleasant the
more they resemble those of art.'[2] Some of the most delightful
descriptive passages in eighteenth-century poetry are therefore

[1] Stopford Brooke, *Naturalism in English Poetry*, 1920, p. 19.
[2] *Spectator*, No. 414.

concerned with the winter landscape, when frost and snow
have combined to give to the trees and the flowers an odd
appearance of artificiality. It was this natural artificiality that
charmed Ambrose Philips one winter (1709) at Copenhagen:

> And yet but lately have I seen, e'en here,
> The winter in a lovely dress appear.
> E'er yet the clouds let fall the treasur'd snow,
> Or winds begun thro' hazy skies to blow.
> At ev'ning a keen eastern breeze arose;
> And the descending rain unsullied froze.
> Soon as the silent shades of night withdrew,
> The ruddy morn disclos'd at once to view
> The face of Nature in a rich disguise,
> And brighten'd ev'ry object to my eyes.
> For ev'ry shrub, and ev'ry blade of grass,
> And ev'ry pointed thorn, seem'd wrought in glass.
> In pearls and rubies rich the hawthorns show,
> While thro' the ice the crimson berries glow.
> The thick-sprung reeds the watry marshes yield,
> Seem polish'd lances in a hostile field.
> The stag in limpid currents with surprize
> Sees chrystal branches on his forehead rise.
> The spreading oak, the beech, and tow'ring pine,
> Glaz'd over, in the freezing æther shine.
> The frighted birds the rattling branches shun,
> That wave and glitter in the distant sun.
>   When if a sudden gust of wind arise,
> The brittle forest into atoms flies:
> The crackling wood beneath the tempest bends,
> And in a spangled show'r the prospect ends. . . .[1]

Cowper, in his 'Winter Morning Walk', notices the 'glittering
turrets' of ice and the 'pillars of pellucid length' formed by the
drops of water as they congeal, and goes on to reflect:

> Thus Nature works as if to mock at Art,
> And in defiance of her rival powers.[2]

Nature mocking delightfully at Art may be seen again in Pope's
description of the woody landscape mirrored in the still waters
of the river Loddon:

> Oft in her glass the musing shepherd spies
> The headlong mountains, and the downward skies,

---

[1] 'A Winter Piece, To the Earl of Dorset', ll. 24 ff. (Chalmers, xiii. 118).
[2] *The Task*, v. 122 f.

The wat'ry landscape of the pendant woods,
And absent trees that tremble in the floods;
In the clear azure gleam the flocks are seen,
And floating forests paint the waves with green. . . .[1]

'Tis Nature still, but Nature so far methodized as to have
become almost a landscape-painting framed in the still depths
of the Loddon: the scene appealed to Pope, we may be sure,
because Nature was here mocking so successfully at Art.

When it comes to placing the human figure in the natural
scene, the eighteenth-century poet often shows an understand-
able fondness for those human activities which most partake of
art.  The angler who 'eyes the dancing cork, and bending reed',
or who seeks more subtly to simulate 'the wanton errors of
the floating fly', is a favourite figure in the eighteenth-century
poetical landscape.  He has that faint unreality which contemporary poets welcomed, he blends easily with the natural
scene at the same time as he—not too seriously—humanizes
it, and he is engaged in a skilful and gentlemanly pursuit, the
perfection of negligent and graceful artifice.  So, too, in Nicholas
Amhurst's 'The Bowling Green' (a translation of Addison's
Latin poem, 'Sphaeristerium') we are allowed to look on at
another delicately artificial activity:

The leader poises in his hand the bowl,
And gently launches to the distant goal:
The current orb prolongs its circling course,
Till by degrees it loses all its force.
When now another o'er the level bounds,
And orb succeeding orb the block surrounds:
Scattered they lie, and barricade the green,
That scarce a single bowl can pass between.
When now with better skill, and nicer care,
The dexterous youth renews the wooden war,
Beyond the rest his winding timber flies,
And works insinuating, and wins the prize.
But if perchance he sees, with madness stung,
The lagging wood move impotent along;
If its faint motion languish on the way,
And, short of length, it press the verdant lay;
Nimbly he strides behind across the grass,
And bending, hovers o'er the rolling mass. . . .[2]

[1] *Windsor Forest*, ll. 211 ff.
[2] *The Works of Joseph Addison* ('Bohn' ed.), 1912, vi. 576 f.

The eye of the poet is fixed steadily enough on his object (he notes how the bowler chafes and 'his body to a thousand postures screws' when his bowl runs wide of the mark); but the bowl so observed is 'the erroneous wood', and the emphasis is all the time on the charming artificiality of the game (the 'wooden war') rather than on its natural setting.

Man, therefore, is the measure of all things in eighteenth-century poetry, and by adapting his mood and treatment to his theme the poet was able to deal with a surprisingly wide range of human actions. From the publication of Thomson's *Seasons*, however, Nature plays a more and more important part in the poet's thoughts, until scenery ends by becoming a spiritual blight on the minor poetry of the nineteenth century.

The determination of many readers of poetry to bring every piece of descriptive writing to the naturalistic test, and to praise or condemn in proportion to the degree of naturalism achieved, is frequently beside the point when applied to the work of the eighteenth-century poet. As often as not he is treating Nature in a purely decorative spirit; and what he does with leaf and twig, bird and beast, may then be compared to the carving of, say, Grinling Gibbons in wood, or to the floral design in a book ornament or in a piece of needlework. The details may, indeed, be true to life, but equally well they may be formalized, and in any case it is the design that matters. When Pope writes, for instance, of the various fish which our plenteous streams supply—

> The bright-ey'd perch with fins of Tyrian dye,
> The silver eel in shining volumes roll'd,
> The yellow carp, in scales bedropp'd with gold,
> Swift trouts, diversified with crimson stains,
> And pikes, the tyrants of the wat'ry plains—[1]

he is not trying to give an exact description of British fish that would enable anyone to identify at once what he had pulled out of the water. The visual effect is, in fact, almost heraldic: we might see such light and such colour in a stained-glass window on a sunny day, or in the arms of the Fishmongers' Company. The auditory effect—and above all the magnificent euphony and voluptuous movement of

> The silver eel in shining volumes roll'd—

[1] *Windsor Forest*, ll. 142 ff.

amplifies the visual effect, and emphasizes the formality of the whole design.

Pope's eel is indeed a poetical eel, an eel that never was on sea or land. He frequently passes in this fashion beyond the actual to some ideal conception of his own:

> Lo where Maeotis sleeps, and hardly flows
> The freezing Tanais thro' a waste of snows.[1]

Pope had never seen the Tanais, he had only read about it. But he knew the Thamesis at Twickenham well enough, and he must often have seen it flowing between snow-covered banks in the winter months. Even so, the effect of this couplet lies less perhaps in its visual than in its auditory effects, and in the suggestion latent in 'sleeps' and 'a waste of snows'. More significantly, the couplet is not to be torn from its context, where it contributes its own special note of numbness and dreariness to a passage dealing with the spread of dullness in the wake of the conquering Vandals.

It is, finally, a noble justification of the contemporary preference for *general* descriptions. Those can sometimes be dull enough; but is the dullness then due to the generalizing process? All writing is tedious when the poet does not feel, or when his words fail to convey what he is feeling. Pope is dull in just that way in some lines at the opening of *Windsor Forest*:

> Here waving groves a chequer'd scene display,
> And part admit, and part exclude the day;
> As some coy nymph her lover's warm address
> Not quite indulges, nor can quite repress.
> There, interspers'd in lawns and op'ning glades,
> Thin trees arise that shun each other's shades.
> Here in full light the russet plains extend:
> There wrapt in clouds the blueish hills ascend.
> Ev'n the wild heath displays her purple dyes,
> And 'midst the desert fruitful fields arise,
> That crown'd with tufted trees and springing corn,
> Like verdant isles the sable waste adorn.

Had Pope written often thus, it would be useless to praise him. The trouble is not that he was not writing with his eye fixed steadily on the object; he was describing a scene that was familiar to him in every detail, and that may have been before his eyes as he wrote. But it was an untidy scene for an early

[1] *The Dunciad*, iii. 87 f.

eighteenth-century poet to describe; it lacked that ordered significance that the poet and the painter normally desired. Pope probably knew this, and his insistence that the landscape around Windsor Forest was '*harmoniously* confused' and that it was one of those in which 'order in variety we see' is perhaps an attempt to justify his description of such a mixed scene. But unity here was obscured by variety, and the whole subordinated to the parts. Worse than that, it was a scene recorded in considerable detail without any of that particularization which could alone have given life to such a description. And lastly it was mere description (apart from the 'coy nymph' who gets so superfluously among Pope's trees); it was a record of things seen, not 'felt in the blood and felt along the heart'. When Pope writes, some fifty lines later, of the desolation that followed the Norman conquest, the effect is altogether different:

> The levell'd towns with weeds lie cover'd o'er;
> The hollow winds thro' naked temples roar;
> Round broken columns clasping ivy twin'd;
> O'er heaps of ruin stalk'd the stately hind;
> The fox obscene to gaping tombs retires,
> And savage howlings fill the sacred quires.

This Pope had never seen with his own eyes. He had seen ivy-covered ruins, no doubt; but he was an Englishman born too late, or too early, to have witnessed such scenes of comprehensive devastation as he described here. He was therefore unembarrassed on this occasion by the actual, and could give free scope to his imagination. What it showed him was a scene of general horror, the crystallized memory of many particular scenes of military devastation—in the Bible, in the *Iliad*, in the *Pharsalia* of Lucan, in the Greek and Latin and modern historians, perhaps in Italian and French paintings, and in much else that he had read and heard about,[1] reflected upon, and imaginatively experienced. At its finest, the general description (of Nature or of anything else) is not achieved by merely leaving out, and still less by not looking steadily at the object, but rather by the distillation of many separate experiences into a sort of poetical cordial.

[1] The lines were written in the midst of a European war, some years before the Peace of Utrecht.

# VIII
## POETRY AS AN ART

### I

A LL through the eighteenth century poetry was regarded as an art: the art of making poems. Coleridge and Shelley, you might almost say, wrote poetry: Dryden and Pope wrote poems. The eighteenth-century poet invariably thought in terms of the poem, the thing to be made; and the critics were always ready to tell him how it should be (or more often, perhaps, how it should have been) written. John Dennis drove the critical nail home with his usual confidence:

In short, poetry is either an art, or whimsy and fanaticism. If it is an art, it follows that it must propose an end to it self, and afterwards lay down proper means for the attaining that end: For this is undeniable, that there are proper means for the attaining of every end, and those proper means in poetry we call the rules.[1]

When poetry is thought of primarily as an art, and not as an imaginative experience which may or may not find expression in words, the emphasis will fall naturally on the finished product—on the substance out of which the poem is made and the way in which that substance has been treated, on the form in which the poem has been cast and the language in which the thoughts and sentiments have been expressed.

In every art, as Dennis says, rules or instructions can be given for securing the desired results. If you want to make oatcakes you must use a girdle and you will bake with a quick flame; if you want to make girdle-scones you will have to bake them on a slower flame. Failure to obtain the proper ingredients (most oatcakes baked in England are made with too fine a meal), or failure to secure the correct conditions for baking, will result in some sort of hybrid—soggy oatcakes, or scones that are done on the outside only—and any good cook will be able to tell on tasting them just what is wrong with them. To the much more complicated art of poetry the trained eighteenth-century reader brought the same sort of experienced judgement. Much more than the twentieth-century reader he knew what to expect, for the effects aimed at by the poets he read were more definite

[1] *Critical Works*, i. 335.

(because subject to general agreement) and limited in number (because poet and reader recognized that there was only a limited number of 'kinds').

## II

The twentieth century has seen the steady deterioration of the old hierarchy of literary Kinds. In the contemporary theatre Tragedy and Comedy have almost ceased to exist as recognizable genres: plays to-day are serious or frivolous, they make an audience laugh or cry (or more probably both), but the literary historian of the future will have difficulty in placing most of them in any well-defined category. The walls that used to separate one kind of literary property from another have been mostly thrown down, and few people at present seem anxious to re-erect them. In the Novel the confusion (or diffusion) is still more noticeable. Even when we find what looks like a distinct genre such as the Detective Story, the boundaries are undefined. Some detective stories concentrate on the crime and its solution as an intellectual problem; others introduce a considerable element of character-study or a love-interest; others, again, base their appeal mainly on a quick succession of exciting adventures. These last are properly 'thrillers', but the contemporary confusion in such matters is borne out by the tendency to use the word 'thriller' to describe any story dealing with a crime and its solution. If the eighteenth century had created the detective story it would quickly have become a recognized Kind, with its own canon and its own rules.

In poetry the absence of Kinds to-day is perhaps still more striking, for there they were once particularly well defined, and now they can scarcely be said to exist at all. It is sometimes thought that twentieth-century poetry is predominantly lyrical, but we can only call most of it so if by 'lyrical' we mean nothing more than 'short'. A break with the established Kinds had already begun with the Romantic poets. Wordsworth's rather unhappy decision to group his poems under such headings as 'Poems of the Fancy', 'Poems of the Imagination', 'Poems proceeding from Sentiment and Reflection', 'Poems on the Naming of Places', 'Ecclesiastical Sonnets', and the like shows how the wind was blowing. Even more significant is his advice to a minor poet, John Abraham Heraud:

You feel strongly; trust to those feelings, and your poem will take its shape and proportions as a tree does from the vital principle that actuates it. I do not think that great poems can be cast in a mould.[1]

It is the same with Coleridge, who contrasts organic form, which shapes and develops from within, with mechanical regularity not necessarily arising out of the properties of the material, 'as when to a mass of wet clay we give whatever shape we wish it to retain when hardened'.[2] On the principle of organic form there may be an infinite number of right forms: if a poem is shaped and developed from within it will grow like a living creature, and the shape it will take must depend upon how the germ or idea grows and expands in the poet's imagination. The poesy of the Romantics is a gum that oozes, and when the flow stops the poem very properly stops with it. Their fondness for such titles as 'Childe Alarique, a Poet's Reverie', 'Rinaldo, the Visionary, a Desultory Poem', 'Extempore, to Walter Scott, Esq.', 'Wallace, a Fragment' (all taken from the work of R. P. Gillies, 1788–1858), besides innumerable 'Lines left upon a Seat' and 'Stanzas written in Dejection', will indicate how little they were accustomed to think in terms of literary Kinds or even of complete poems. Coleridge and Shelley were both fertile in the production of 'Fragments', for neither would write on when the original impulse had died. With many of the minor Romantics, on the other hand, the Fragment became a conscious exercise in the incomplete, in much the same fashion as ruined temples and crumbling hermitages were erected in the landscape gardens of their grandfathers. The deliberate publication of a 'Fragment' would have seemed to Pope or Johnson an intolerable liberty to take with the public; they would no more have thought of publishing an uncompleted poem than of publishing the first two acts of a play.

The eighteenth-century poet set out to write not only a poem rather than poetry, but a poem which belonged to one of the recognized Kinds.

There were [it has been said] exact patterns of different kinds of poetry laid up in some heaven to which the true scholar might rise in his contemplations. . . . What influence these ideal patterns had, what reverence they evoked, is scarcely conceivable now.[3]

---

[1] *The Letters of William and Dorothy Wordsworth: The Later Years*, ed. E. De Selincourt, p. 537.

[2] *Lectures and Notes on Shakespeare*, ed. T. Ashe ('Bohn' ed.), p. 229.

[3] W. P. Ker, Introduction to Dryden, *Essays*, i, p. xv f.

The poet knew beforehand the sort of achievement possible in each Kind and the type of treatment required,[1] and he was well aware what had been done in it by previous writers.

At the top of the hierarchy, the king of all the literary beasts, was the Epic, supported by an immense body of critical theory. Indeed, so important was the Epic in the scheme of things that the neo-classical critics sometimes extended to all poetry rules which were applicable only to the heroic poem. There were many other Kinds, great and small; each had an appropriate range of subjects and a style suited to it, each was capable of its own peculiar excellence.

There is little in the poetry of Pope that does not belong to one or other of the recognized Kinds. He began, as poets had traditionally begun, with Pastorals, and lest there should be any doubt about his own conscious attempt to write them correctly he prefixed to them a Discourse on Pastoral Poetry. In his *Essay on Criticism* he passed on to another Kind, the familiar discourse on poetry in the manner of Horace's *Ars Poetica*. *The Rape of the Lock*, like *The Dunciad* sixteen years later, was an exercise in the Mock-heroic, which again had a respectable literary lineage going back to the *Batrachomyomachia*, and which was carefully distinguished from its poor relation, the Burlesque. *Windsor Forest* was Pope's venture in a comparatively recent Kind, the 'local' poem, which can trace its ancestry no farther back than Sir John Denham's *Cooper's Hill* (1642). He had his Elegy ('To the Memory of an Unfortunate Lady'), his Heroic Epistle (*Eloisa to Abelard*), and his various imitations of the familiar Epistles of Horace. He wrote Prologues, Epitaphs, Epigrams, and Odes. He did not write an epic poem, but he translated two; and he told Spence, 'I should certainly have written an Epic Poem, if I had not engaged in the translation of Homer.'[2] He had thought, too, of trying his hand at 'a Persian fable; in which I should have given a full loose to description and imagination. It would have been a very wild thing, if I had executed it.'[3] It is characteristic of Pope that even when he is contemplating a departure from the normal poetry of his age he is already planning a new Kind, a cross between the Persian Tales and Dryden's Fables.

---

[1] Cf. Boileau, *L'Art poétique*, ii. 115: 'Tout poème est brillant de sa propre beauté.'
[2] Spence, *Anecdotes*, p. 259.
[3] Ibid., p. 140.

The extent to which categories or Kinds dominated the outlook of the century may be seen again in painting. To Reynolds
the highest reach to which his art can attain is 'history-painting',
which corresponds in his view with the epic in poetry; it paints
man in general, avoiding the minute and particular and aiming
always at the ideal. There are, however, other Kinds: portrait-
painting, landscape-painting, 'the French gallantries of Wat-
teau', the representation of low and vulgar life (Hogarth,
Teniers, &c.), animal-painting, and so on. The artists in those
other, but inferior, Kinds 'have, in general, the same right, in
different degrees, to the name of a painter, which a satirist, an
epigrammatist, a sonnetteer, a writer of pastorals or descriptive
poetry, has to that of a poet'.[1] Each Kind has its own rules, and
the painter will do well or badly in his own genre according as
he observes or neglects those rules.

This constant tendency to think in Kinds was due in part to
the formalism of an age which never felt more comfortable than
when it was formally dressed, and in part to a widespread conservatism which amounted at times to a spiritual timidity.
You knew where you were with Pastoral, Elegy, Epic, and the
rest; you were not called upon to adjust yourself to the untried
or the unexpected.

Even in the eighteenth century, however, men were not
willing to bask for ever in the traditional perfections. Repetition
cloyed the effect, and some sort of innovation became inevitable.
The characteristic compromise was to seek variety within the
established form: not to abandon the known Kinds, but to
introduce a slight change of subject or treatment. The Pastoral,
for example, could hardly have survived as a living form if the
poets had done nothing more than echo Pope. In fact they kept
it alive by frequent blood-transfusion. Apart from Gay's burlesque in *The Shepherd's Week*, there were mild and pleasing
innovations (mild enough to avoid all risk of confusing any-
body) such as Diaper's *Nereides; or Sea Eclogues* (1712), Lady
Mary Wortley Montagu's *Town Eclogues*, and Collins's *Persian
Eclogues* (1742). Pope, too, had considered a possible development of the Pastoral poem—'American pastorals, or rather
pastorals adapted to the manners of several of the ruder nations,
as well as the Americans'.[2] A minor poetical fashion was started

---

[1] *Discourses*, pp. 38, 114, 177 f.
[2] Spence, *Anecdotes*, p. 140.

by Nicholas Rowe about 1712 with his Pastoral Ballad of 'Colin's Complaint':

> Despairing beside a clear stream,
>   A shepherd forsaken was laid;
> And while a false nymph was his theme,
>   A willow supported his head.
> The wind that blew over the plain,
>   To his sighs with a sigh did reply;
> And the brook, in return to his pain,
>   Ran mournfully murmuring by.

Rowe's pleasant lines were imitated by various writers, most notably by Shenstone in his 'Pastoral Ballad', and parodied by (among others) Lady Mary Wortley Montagu. It was not merely the lilting measure of 'Colin's Complaint' that was imitated (though that, no doubt, was its strongest appeal), but the pretty mixed sentiment, at once natural and delicately sophisticated, which led one of the poet's contemporaries to refer to him as 'soft, complaining Rowe'. No better illustration could be found of the eighteenth-century habit of holding on to what had once pleased. Rowe had produced, by a sort of cross-fertilization, a new poetical flower, and later writers continued to cultivate it. Not all such hybrids were equally successful. Shenstone, for instance, wrote what he called a 'Pastoral Ode', but this particular sport never established itself in the poetical catalogue. Many other minor Kinds were silently admitted without ever being clearly defined. The Prospect Poem was one of those, and the Night Piece another. For the eighteenth century the Night Piece probably began with Lady Winchilsea's 'Nocturnal Reverie' (1713); it was developed by Parnell ('A Night Piece on Death') and by a number of later writers. Young's *Night Thoughts* may perhaps be regarded as the little Night Piece writ large, though Young's poem belongs rather to the sphere of rhapsody and ejaculation. The Night Piece was a loose and accommodating form (the word 'piece' almost disarms criticism), but it may be described as a nocturna reverie, solemn or at least written in sober sadness, often (but not necessarily) connected with death, and sometimes located in a graveyard. It is the poetry of solitude and low spirits, tinged with melancholy and sustained by a contemplative resignation; the stillness of the night tends to sharpen the poet's senses, and the mystery of the darkness to quicken his imagination.

Sometimes the Kind was of old and respectable ancestry, but no critic had troubled to define it. In *Spectator*, No. 618, an unidentified contributor offers some critical remarks on the verse Epistle. 'This is a species of poetry by itself,' he observes, 'and has not so much as been hinted at in any of the arts of poetry that have ever fallen into my hands.' He proceeds to repair the omission, subdividing his Kind into two classes: the Ovidian (love-letters, letters of friendship, &c.) and the Horatian (familiar, critical, and moral epistles), and stating what qualifications are needed by the writer of each class, and what sort of effect he must aim at. Thus for the Horatian epistle the writer must have plenty of strong masculine sense, a thorough knowledge of mankind and of the prevailing humours of the age, and a sound morality. As for style, he must not have the air of a recluse, but of a man of the world; he should be a master of refined raillery, well versed in the delicacies and absurdities of conversation, free and disengaged in manner, and well able to draw on common life for his illustrations and comparisons. Similarly, in *Guardian*, No. 16, Steele undertakes to define the Song ('I do not remember ever to have met with any piece of criticism upon this subject'). For songs (he says) no great knowledge or elevation of thought is required of the writer; but they do demand the utmost nicety and regularity. They should be easy and flowing, elegant but unaffected, with one uniform and simple design. Above all, they must be quite perfect; the slightest blemish, like a flaw in a jewel, destroys the effect. The best models are to be found in Sappho, Anacreon, and Horace, and, among modern nations, the French poets. Thus instructed, Steele's readers could go ahead more confidently with the writing of songs.

Sometimes the new Kind arrived more suddenly, and we can watch the almost biological progress of its growth and formulation. Something of this sort happened with Opera. In 1685 Dryden wrote a Preface for his opera, *Albion and Albanius*, in which he undertook to settle the chief features of this comparatively new Kind from such examples as were then available.

The first inventors of any art or science [he wrote], provided they have brought it to perfection, are, in reason, to give laws to it; and, according to their model, all after-undertakers are to build.

We do not dispute the authority of Homer in Epic, or of Pindar in the Ode, and anyone essaying to write Opera 'is obliged to imitate the design of the Italians, who have . . . brought to perfection this sort of dramatic musical entertainment'. And so Dryden proceeds, very much after Aristotle's inductive method, to pronounce upon the type of subject proper to Opera (it goes beyond the limits of human nature, and 'admits of that sort of marvellous and surprising conduct which is re-jected in other plays'); the persons who ought to be represented (gods, goddesses, and heroes descended from them, but also— in view of Guarini's *Pastor Fido*—'meaner persons', who 'may sometimes gracefully be introduced, especially if they have relation to those first times which poets call the Golden Age)'; the language (which ought to be soft, sweet, and harmonious like the Italian); the metre and the rhyme; the scenes, machines, and dancing.[1] It is clear that Dryden feels no special pride in being an innovator; he would just as soon that the rules for Opera had been laid down once and for all. To Dryden, as to Pope after him, the pleasure of writing came not from a sense of complete freedom, but rather from a consciousness of common form which could be varied and modified to suit his purpose. Writer and reader had become accustomed to the Kind, and they felt a sense of loss or confusion if they were unable to place a poem. Something of this feeling probably accounts for Swift's dissatisfaction with Thomson's *Seasons*. Writing in 1732 to a friend about the use of blank verse in poetry, he remarks:

One Thomson, a Scotchman, has succeeded the best in that way, in four poems he has writ on the four seasons, yet I am not over fond of them, because they are all description, and nothing is doing, whereas Milton engages me in actions of the highest importance, *modo me Romae, modo ponit Athenis*, . . .[2]

Thomson's *Seasons*, mainly descriptive, was not yet one of the recognized Kinds: to the conservative Swift a long poem should have a fable, an action of some sort. He would probably have felt more at home with the *Seasons* if Thomson had cast his poem in the form of Virgil's *Georgics*.

III

Since the division of poetry into its various Kinds was not just a pedantic classification made by critics after the poem was

<hr>

[1] *Essays*, i. 271 ff.                    [2] *Correspondence*, ed. F. E. Ball, iv. 330.

written, but one which the poet was fully conscious of while he
wrote, we should be prepared to see the Kind exercising some
degree of pressure on the expression. Whether we do see it or
not, that is almost always happening with the best poets of the
period; and it is, in fact, one aspect of Correctness. If we are not
nearly so conscious of those ńuances as the contemporary
reader was, the explanation must be that the whole poetic
idiom of the eighteenth century is strange to us and we are
therefore less likely to be alive to subtle modifications from one
poem to another. Yet any attentive reader must perceive a wide
difference between the diction of, say, the *Epistle to Dr. Arbuthnot* and Pope's *Homer*, and any sensitive reader should feel a
more subtle difference between the diction (and the rhythm)
of his *Pastorals*—

> For her the flocks refuse their verdant food,
> Nor thirsty heifers seek the gliding flood.
> The silver swans her hapless fate bemoan,
> In notes more sad than when they sing their own;
> In hollow caves sweet Echo silent lies,
> Silent, or only to her name replies;
> Her name with pleasure once she taught the shore,
> Now Daphne's dead, and pleasure is no more[1]—

and of the *Elegy to the Memory of an Unfortunate Lady*—

> What can atone (oh ever-injur'd shade!)
> Thy fate unpity'd, and thy rites unpaid?
> No friend's complaint, no kind domestic tear
> Pleas'd thy pale ghost, or grac'd thy mournful bier;
> By foreign hands thy dying eyes were clos'd,
> By foreign hands thy decent limbs compos'd,
> By foreign hands thy humble grave adorn'd,
> By strangers honour'd, and by strangers mourn'd![2]

or of *Eloisa to Abelard*—

> Far other dreams my erring soul employ,
> Far other raptures, of unholy joy:
> When at the close of each sad, sorrowing day,
> Fancy restores what vengeance snatch'd away,
> Then conscience sleeps, and leaving nature free,
> All my loose soul unbounded springs to thee.
> O curst, dear horrors of all-conscious night!
> How glowing guilt exalts the keen delight!

---

[1] 'Winter', ll. 37 ff.                                   [2] ll. 47 ff.

Provoking Daemons all restraint remove,
And stir within me ev'ry source of love.
I hear thee, view thee, gaze o'er all thy charms,
And round thy phantom glue my clasping arms.[1]

The melodious lament of the first, the controlled grief of
the second, and the uncontrolled (or, more accurately, de-
controlled) passion of the last piece are perhaps achieved mainly
by the poet's delicate mastery of his rhythms, but the diction,
too, responds to a change of mood and intention. With such a
poet as Pope it would be naïve to suggest that any one of those
three pieces is less artificial than another; but superficially, at
least, the diction of the passage from the *Pastorals* is more artificial than that of the others because to Pope the Pastoral is 'an
image of what they call the golden age' and not of shepherds
'as shepherds at this day really are'.[2] In the *Elegy*, if the diction
is not quite 'the language of the heart', it is the language of a
grief more fully imagined and more deeply contemplated than
that of Thyrsis mourning for Daphne; it is not, nor is it intended
to be, the language of a private sorrow but of a celebration as
public as a funeral, and as dignified. In *Eloisa to Abelard*, where,
it has been said, 'the feelings of mankind become strange
because they have become extreme' and 'the operatic flights
outdo the rhetoric of Ovid',[3] Pope is attempting the language of
a heart torn by conflicting passions. The eighteenth-century
reader was accustomed to hearing something of the kind when
he visited Drury Lane or Covent Garden, though never perhaps
among Pope's contemporaries did it reach such splendour and
animation.

Even in his own day (and this may be some comfort to the
twentieth-century reader) the poet could not always count
upon an adequate response to the subtleties of his diction.
Dryden on one occasion expressed his annoyance with those of
his readers who were too obtuse to realize that there was not
*one* style suitable to poetry, but many.

Some who have seen a paper of verses which I wrote last year to
her Highness the Duchess, have accused them of that only thing I
could defend in them. They said, I did *humi serpere*,—that I wanted
not only height of fancy, but dignity of words, to set it off. I might

[1] ll. 223 ff.
[2] 'A Discourse on Pastoral Poetry', prefixed to the *Pastorals*.
[3] *The Poems of Alexander Pope* ('Twickenham' ed.), ed. G. Tillotson, ii. 290.

well answer with that of Horace, *Nunc non erat his locus*; I knew I
addressed them to a lady, and accordingly I affected the softness of
expression, and the smoothness of measure, rather than the height
of thought; and in what I did endeavour, it is no vanity to say I have
succeeded.[1]

Pope gave just as much thought—perhaps more—to those delicacies of expression. Talking of his *Pastorals* on one occasion,
he observed:

Though Virgil, in his pastorals, has sometimes six or eight lines
together that are epic, I have been so scrupulous as scarce ever to
admit above two together, even in the Messiah.[2]

And on another occasion:

After writing a poem, one should correct it all over, with one
single view at a time. Thus for language; if an elegy; 'these lines are
very good, but are they not of too heroical a strain?' and so *vice versa*.[3]

In view of Pope's sensitive adjustment of sound and rhythm and
vocabulary to his meaning it is not surprising to find him complaining pessimistically: 'I scarce meet with any body that
understands delicacy.'[4]  Still, the eighteenth-century reader,
who read for the most part the poetry of his own century, was
in a better position than we are to-day to respond quickly to
modulations within the heroic couplet, to change of pace,
variety of texture, and significant changes in diction, because (unlike us) he was so familiar with the norm. But if the
twentieth-century reader starts at a disadvantage, he need not
be sceptical merely because his own ear sometimes fails to
record any results.

IV

To say that in eighteenth-century poetry the diction varied
from one kind of poem to another is not to deny that there was
at this period a recognized poetic diction upon which the poets
consciously drew. In the gradual crystallization of this special
diction two stages may perhaps be distinguished: (1) certain
words and phrases are not suited to poetry because they are too
'low', i.e. too colloquial, too much associated with particular
trades or professions, too prosaic and everyday, and so on.
Such words and phrases must therefore be avoided. (2) Certain

---

[1] *Essays*, i. 18 f.                    [2] Spence, *Anecdotes*, p. 312.
[3] Ibid., p. 23 f.                       [4] Ibid., p. 265.

words and phrases have come to be peculiarly associated with poetry. Those words and phrases should therefore be chosen since they are 'poetical', and poetry is something written in poetic diction. No genuine poet would have thought of expressing the second stage in the development so crudely as that, but most of them were conscious of a poetic value resting in the purely literary associations of certain words. The words themselves were so many poetic units.

The first, or negative, stage was about as far as Dryden had cared to go. Though he wished poetry to be written in the language of gentlemen, he was still thinking rather of excluding words that failed to pass the test of propriety and elegance than of restricting poets to a specialized vocabulary. But is that quite how Pope saw the problem? In his satirical and familiar poetry he is free enough, but in his translation of Homer he seems to have passed on to the second, or positive, stage. Johnson's comment on the language of Pope's *Homer* is significant:

. . . there is scarcely a happy combination of words or a phrase poetically elegant in the English language which Pope has not inserted into his version of Homer. How he obtained possession of so many beauties of speech it were desirable to know. That he gleaned from authors, obscure as well as eminent, what he thought brilliant or useful, and preserved it all in a regular collection, is not unlikely. When, in his last years, Hall's *Satires* were shewn him he wished that he had seen them sooner.[1]

Beside this passage we may put another from Johnson's 'Life of Dryden':

There was therefore before the time of Dryden no poetical diction: no system of words at once refined from the grossness of domestick use and free from the harshness of terms appropriated to particular arts. . . . Those happy combinations of words which distinguish poetry from prose had been rarely attempted; we had few elegances or flowers of speech: the roses had not yet been plucked from the bramble or different colours had not yet been joined to enliven one another.[2]

The implication of those two passages is sufficiently clear: certain words and phrases and turns of expression are eminently striking and poetical; it is those that a poet should employ. Indeed, he will show his knowledge of the poetic art by the

[1] *Lives*, iii. 251.                    [2] Ibid. i. 420.

extent to which he does make use of them. But where is he to
find them? Chiefly in the works of earlier (but not too early)
poets who have taken the risk of introducing them into poetry,
where they are now safely established.[1] No one put it quite so
simply as that, but most of the poets and critics thought along
those lines. It is in much the same spirit that the schoolboy
writes his Latin prose, well aware that a good prose is one into
which he can introduce a *quae cum ita sint* and a *haud multum
abfuit quin*, and (if fortune favours him) a *quippe qui*. There is,
of course, no question of his striking any new Latin phrases for
himself; if he does, the less of a latinist he. His duty is always
to follow the best models. As a schoolboy, he is not likely to
have contaminated his style by reading any of the late Latin
writers; but if he had read, say, Tertullian he would no more
think of imitating Tertullian's style than Pope would have
thought of writing like Marston or Chapman. When, therefore,
Johnson says of Pope that 'he has left in his *Homer* a treasure of
poetical elegances to posterity',[2] he is thinking not merely of
future generations of readers enjoying those elegances, but also
of future generations of poets making further use of them.

By the middle of the eighteenth century English poetry had
acquired a vocabulary which had almost become a second
language.

The language of the age [Gray told his friend West] is never the
language of poetry; except among the French, whose verse, where
the thought or image does not support it, differs in nothing from
prose. Our poetry, on the contrary, has a language peculiar to itself;
to which almost every one that has written has added something, by
enriching it with foreign idioms and derivatives: Nay, sometimes
words of their own composition or invention.[3]

Gray goes on to note that Shakespeare and Milton have been
'great creators this way', and that Dryden and Pope have
borrowed from them in turn. Gray himself borrowed from all
four, and his poetry illustrates perfectly the way in which an
eighteenth-century poet willingly availed himself of 'happy
combinations of words' and 'phrases poetically elegant in the
English language'. When he wrote the lines,

---

[1] Or in such compilations as Joshua Poole's *The English Parnassus: or a Help to
English Poesie . . . with all the choicest epithets and phrases, with some General Forms upon all
Occasions, Subjects and Themes . . .*, 1657.
[2] *Lives*, iii. 238.                                    [3] *Correspondence*, i. 192.

Full many a flower is born to blush unseen,
And waste its sweetness on the desert air

the thought was of a kind that might have occurred independently to any poet in any age. But Gray must have known
Pope's

Like roses that in deserts bloom and die[1]

and (blushing almost unseen in Ambrose Philips's *Thule*) he
might have found:

Like woodland flowers, which paint the desert glades,
And waste their sweets in unfrequented shades.

If Gray was indebted to Pope, Pope in his turn was pretty
certainly recalling Waller's lines in 'Go, lovely rose':

Tell her that's young,
And shuns to have her graces spied,
That hadst thou sprung
In deserts, where no men abide,
Thou must have uncommended died—

and it is just possible that he may have remembered two lines in
William Chamberlayne's *Pharonnida*:

Like beauteous flowers which vainly waste the scent
Of odours in unhaunted deserts . . . .[2]

Some ten years after the appearance of Philips's *Thule* (1718)
Young wrote in his *Universal Passion*:

In distant wilds, by human eyes unseen,
She rears her flow'rs, and spreads her velvet green;
Pure gurgling rills the lonely desart trace,
And waste their music on the savage race.[3]

Gray had almost certainly read those lines, and they may have
been stirring in the back of his mind with the other echoes.

His own lines in the *Elegy* are perhaps finer than any of the
earlier passages which may have suggested them: if not finer,
they are at least different in effect. The question of literary
borrowing was one to which eighteenth-century poets and
critics gave a good deal of thought. The young Pope aired his
views on the subject to his elderly friend Walsh:

I would beg your opinion, too, as to another point: it is how far

[1] *The Rape of the Lock*, iv. 158.
[2] *Minor Poets of the Caroline Period*, ed. G. Saintsbury, i. 232.
[3] v. 229 ff.

the liberty of borrowing may extend? I have defended it sometimes by saying, that it seems not so much the perfection of sense to say things that had never been said before, as to express those best that have been said oftenest; and that writers, in the case of borrowing from others, are like trees, which of themselves would produce only one sort of fruit, but by being grafted upon others may yield variety. A mutual commerce makes poetry flourish; but then poets, like merchants, should repay with something of their own what they take from others; not, like pirates, make prize of all they meet. I desire you to tell me sincerely, if I have not stretched this license too far in these Pastorals.[1]

Walsh was reassuring:

Indeed, in all the common subjects of poetry, the thoughts are so obvious, at least if they are natural, that whoever writes last must write things like what have been said before.[2]

The eighteenth-century reader was well aware that some second-rate writers were mere plagiaries; but there was no widespread feeling against imitation, no tendency to point scornfully at some passage and say, 'This is simply lifted from Dryden', or 'He got that from *The Rape of the Lock*'. On the contrary, so long as the poet passed Pope's test and repaid with something of his own, his imitations were counted as poetical assets. The poet himself rarely showed any anxiety to conceal his poetical borrowings, and indeed was often at some pains to point them out to the reader. In the Preface to his *Annus Mirabilis* Dryden not only acknowledges but even boasts of his debt to Virgil:

I have followed him everywhere, I know not with what success, but I am sure with diligence enough; my images are many of them copied from him, and the rest are imitations of him. My expressions also are as near as the idioms of the two languages would admit of in translation.[3]

This is as much as to say: 'I don't know what you will think of my poem, but I can guarantee that it is made out of good sound materials. It is the very best Virgil.' Pope, too, pointed out many, though by no means all, of his imitations of earlier writers.[4] Even when a poet repaid with little or nothing of his own he was ready to justify his borrowings on the grounds that

---

[1] *Works*, ed. Elwin–Courthope, vi. 52 (2 July 1706).
[2] Ibid. 53 (20 July 1706).                    [3] *Essays*, i. 17.
[4] Mr. Eliot has revived this practice in 'The Waste Land'.

allusion was itself pleasurable. So in 1713 we find one John Smith, the author of a volume of *Poems upon Several Occasions*, informing his readers:

> To avoid the imputation of a plagiary, I have printed whatsoever I have taken from any English writer as far as my memory could go back, in a distinct character. . . . Such fragments as these, serve for a kind of inlay to the work, and afford a graceful variety.

Nothing could be more chilling to the modern reader than to come upon a passage in 'a distinct character' or in inverted commas because the poet had lifted a few words from Keats or Tennyson.

The argument of Walsh that 'whoever writes last must write things like what have been said before' will not serve to explain every kind of borrowing in the eighteenth century. The borrowing frequently occurs when the material borrowed is by no means common; but to the eighteenth-century poet what had once appeared in poetry was common property, and could be used again. The poetical fortune of the word 'calenture' will throw some light on the neo-classical tendency to employ material already used, and to vary upon the existing pattern rather than startle the reader with something entirely unfamiliar. The word itself seems to have come into the language towards the end of the sixteenth century, and no doubt gained currency then because of the experiences of Elizabethan sailors in tropical seas. The calenture is 'a disease incident to sailors within the tropics, characterized by delirium in which the patient, it is said, fancies the sea to be green fields, and desires to leap into it' (*O.E.D.*). It seems to have been associated, too, with calms, when the sun's rays beat upon the ocean and the ship lay motionless in the water. It is in these circumstances that we meet with it in 'The Calme' of Donne:

> Onely the calenture together drawes
> Deare friends, which meet dead in great fishes jawes. . . .

The distracted sailor plunging into the ocean supplied the poets with a picturesque image for all sorts of mental delusions. So Almahide replies to the passionate wooing of Almanzor in *The Conquest of Granada* (1670):

> These are the day-dreams which wild fancy yields,
> Empty as shadows are, that fly o'er fields.
> Oh, whither would this boundless fancy move!

> 'Tis but the raging calenture of love.
> Like a distracted passenger you stand,
> And see, in seas, imaginary land,
> Cool groves, and flowery meads; and while you think
> To walk, plunge in, and wonder that you sink.[1]

Twenty years later, in *Don Sebastian*, the same image came to Dryden's mind when his Alvarez addresses another too passionate lover:

> Know, sir, I would be silent if I durst:
> But if, on shipboard, I should see my friend
> Grown frantic in a raging calenture,
> And he, imagining vain flowery fields,
> Would headlong plunge himself into the deep,—
> Should I not hold him from the mad attempt,
> Till his sick fancy were by reason cured?[2]

In Nicholas Rowe's first play, *The Ambitious Stepmother*, which has many echoes of Dryden, we come upon the calenture again in a speech of Cleone:

> But whither does my roving fancy wander?
> These are the sick dreams of fantastick love.
> So in the calenture the seaman fancies
> Green fields and flow'ry meadows on the ocean,
> Till leaping in, the wretch is lost for ever.[3]

Twenty years later, writing of the South Sea Bubble, Swift naturally associates the madness of the speculation with the delirium of sailors in tropical (i.e. South) seas:

> So, by a calenture misled,
> The mariner with rapture sees
> On the smooth ocean's azure bed
> Enamell'd fields, and verdant trees.
>
> With eager hast he longs to rove
> In that fantastick scene, and thinks
> It must be some enchanted grove,
> And in he leaps, and down he sinks.[4]

In a case like this it becomes idle to inquire who borrowed from whom: the calenture had clearly become a part of the common stock of poetical material. It had passed its tests, and was now ready for anyone who wished to use it.[5]

[1] Pt. II. II. iii. 77 ff.          [2] v. i. 215 ff.          [3] III. i. 108 ff.
[4] *The Poems of Jonathan Swift*, ed. Harold Williams, 1937, i. 251 f.
[5] It was to appear again in Cowper's *Task* ('The Sofa', 447 ff.) and in Words-

## V

An age which holds that there is a wide gap separating poetry from prose will have to justify this belief either by producing poetry of a highly imaginative order or else by finding some other way of emphasizing the difference. But the average eighteenth-century poet was a very reasonable sort of person; he was moved by natural human feelings and he had those other feelings proper to the artist working in his own chosen medium, but he rarely showed any outstanding qualities of imagination. How, then, was he to differentiate his poetic utterance from his prose? He did so mainly by the use of poetic diction.

There were several good reasons why the poets of the period found themselves being continually propelled towards the use of this diction. In the first place much of their poetry was written in the heroic couplet, a measure which tends to gene-rate an unusual amount of energy. The tendency of twentieth-century poets has been to move away from the emphatic beat of a regular metre and to turn rather to much quieter and more colloquial rhythms, which in their turn encourage quieter and more colloquial expression. The effect of metre (as Coleridge observed) is to arouse expectation in the reader, and to 'in-crease the vivacity and susceptibility . . . of the general feelings':[1] when, therefore, the metre is irregular and unemphatic, little expectation is aroused and the feelings are less fully engaged. The last English poets of any importance who habitually used the traditional and regular metres are perhaps Kipling and Housman, and it is significant that in both the feeling is fre-quently rhetorical and the diction is of the kind that is most apt to generate such feeling. At all events, the heroic couplet of the eighteenth-century poets, by making an unusually strong demand upon the reader's attention, forced the poet to respond with a language that would not disappoint the expectations aroused.

Ideally, no doubt, this would have been the language of feeling. But if the poet's subject was not itself charged with emotion. he had either to provide the emotion himself or else

worth's 'The Brothers' (60 ff.). Wordsworth's description of the calenture was 'sketched from an imperfect recollection of an admirable one in prose, by Mr. [William] Gilbert, author of *The Hurricane*'.

[1] *Biographia Literaria*, ii. 51.

K

induce it in his readers by means of an artificial diction.[1] Contemporary critics frequently praised the poet who could make a prosaic theme glow and glitter by the use of poetical ornament. To Dryden, Virgil's *Georgics* were 'the divinest part of all his writings' because Virgil had turned into poetry the most unpromising materials, which

are neither great in themselves, nor have any natural ornament to bear them up; but the words wherewith he describes them are so excellent, that it might well be applied to him, which was said by Ovid, *Materiam superabat opus.*[2]

Addison praised the *Georgics* for the same reason; they were a triumph of successful heightening:

He delivers the meanest of his precepts with a kind of grandeur, he breaks the clods and tosses the dung about with an air of gracefulness.[3]

When William Mason undertook in his *English Garden* to inform readers how to erect a fence that should remain invisible, he admitted the difficulty of conveying such instruction in poetry, but he explained how—for the eighteenth-century reader at least—it could be done:

> Ingrateful sure,
> When such the theme, becomes the poet's task:
> Yet must he try, by modulation meet
> Of varied cadence, and selected phrase,
> Exact yet free, without inflation bold,
> To dignify that theme, must try to form
> Such magic sympathy of sense with sound
> As pictures all it sings; while grace awakes
> At each blest touch, and, on the lowliest things,
> Scatters her rainbow hues.[4]

'Ingrateful' perhaps; but the eighteenth-century poet seems often to have got a lot of quiet enjoyment from dignifying the theme. So Cowper, explaining how to prepare a bed for the cucumber frame, refers to the manure as 'a stercoraceous heap' and 'the agglomerated pile'; the frame itself must 'front the sun's meridian disk'; and when all is completed,

> Thrice must the voluble and restless earth
> Spin round upon her axle, ere the warmth,

---

[1] See Note M, p. 170.    [2] *Essays*, i. 16 f.
[3] *The Miscellaneous Works of Joseph Addison*, ed. A. C. Guthkelch, 1914, ii. 9.
[4] Chalmers, xviii. 385.

Slow gathering in the midst, through the square mass
Diffused, attain the surface; when, behold!
A pestilent and most corrosive steam,
Like a gross fog Boeotian, rising fast,
And fast condensed upon the dewy sash,
Asks egress. . . .[1]

If Cowper does this sort of thing with a smile on his face, some eighteenth-century poets were more serious. Boswell recounts the story of how the poet Grainger caused a loud laugh at Sir Joshua Reynolds's house when, reading from the manuscript of his *Sugar Cane*, he suddenly startled the company by saying,

Now, Muse, let's sing of rats. . . .[2]

The objection here, as in many other such examples, is to the mixture of styles; the rats would have been harmless enough if they had not appeared in the company of the Muse. But to the eighteenth-century reader they would still have been, merely as rats, ludicrous in poetry; and Grainger was only complying with the taste of his age when, in revision, he tried to disguise them in a periphrasis:

Nor with less waste the whisker'd vermin race,
A countless clan, despoil the low-land cane.[3]

Such periphrases cushioned the eighteenth-century reader on many occasions from too sharp a contact with actuality. But the periphrasis had several other uses; it might introduce an elegant variation, or it might indicate unemphatically to the reader which of all the varied aspects of a subject he was to concentrate upon (cf. Thomson's 'soft fearful people' for the sheep about to be dipped).[4] Or again, in Dyer's

. . . prickly bramble white with woolly theft[5]

—if 'woolly theft' can still be looked upon as a periphrasis—it could concentrate much meaning in a single phrase. It remains true, however, that the most frequent reason for the periphrasis in eighteenth-century poetry is the poet's feeling that he must keep up the level of utterance. If hens in poetry were going to make people smile (as in Thomson's day they

[1] *The Task*, iii. 490 ff.                                [2] Boswell, *Life*, ii. 453.
[3] *The Sugar Cane*, ii. 62 f. (Chalmers, xiv. 491).
[4] For a fuller discussion of this question, see Geoffrey Tillotson, *Essays in Criticism and Research*, 1942, pp. 53 ff.
[5] *The Fleece*, i. 103 (Chalmers, xiii. 229).

almost inevitably were) the poet did well to avoid the word.
If 'feather'd tribes domestic' makes the twentieth-century
reader feel that Thomson's cure was worse than the disease, we
must accept once more a 'shift of sensibility' and, if we must
smile, smile benignly.

In defending Pope's version of Homer Johnson undertook to
answer those who objected that Pope had failed to reproduce
the spirit of the Greek poet. Homer is simple, artless, unaffected;
Pope's translation (they say) is artificial. Perhaps it is, Johnson
admits; but we must make allowance for a large change in taste
in the course of two thousand years. Even Virgil, who lived not
very long after Homer, wrote quite differently; he found even
then 'the state of the world so much altered, and the demand
for elegance so much increased, that mere nature would be
endured no longer'. In a community just emerging from bar-
barism literature is so new, and the minds of men are so little
instructed, that 'plain sense' is enough to give delight; but

repletion generates fastidiousness, a saturated intellect soon becomes
luxurious, and knowledge finds no willing reception till it be recommended by artificial diction.[1]

This argument of Johnson's is perhaps more dependent on time
and place than he realized; he did not foresee that taste might
shift again towards a much less sophisticated and artificial kind
of literature, though Percy's *Reliques* (1765) and other literary
straws were already showing how the wind was beginning to
blow.

It is true that many of the ornamental effects in eighteenth-
century poetry were there simply because they had become
customary; the reader liked them, and he would have felt that
the poem was too bare without them.

> There see the clover, pea, and bean,
> Vie in variety of green,
> Fresh pastures speckled o'er with sheep,
> Brown fields their fallow sabbaths keep,
> Plump Ceres golden tresses wear,
> And poppy-topknots deck her hair,
> And silver streams thro' meadows stray,
> And Naiads on the margin play,
> And lesser nymphs on side of hills
> From play-thing urns pour down the rills.[2]

[1] *Lives*, iii. 239.          [2] Matthew Green, *The Spleen* (Chalmers, xv. 168).

If Wordsworth had happened to select this passage for critical
comment, he would almost certainly, after his fashion, have
given some sort of approval to the first four lines and condemned the rest outright as another example of 'vicious poetic
diction'. But the contemporary reader no doubt welcomed
Ceres and the Naiads as a necessary relief from 'the clover, pea,
and bean'—good things in their way, but, poetically, little
better than kitchen-stuff. Fifty years later the Naiads are still
performing their modest service to eighteenth-century poetry.
When Cowper writes of a little stream in the neighbourhood
of Olney, a little Naiad dutifully pours her urn for him:

> Hence the declivity is sharp and short,
> And such the reascent; between them weeps
> A little Naiad her impoverished urn
> All summer long, which winter fills again.[1]

Cowper's Naiad does not bring us any closer to the *actuality* of
the stream; indeed, his mode of expression here has the opposite
effect. If we want to get what Keats would have called the 'feel'
of a stream we could not do better than go to his own lines in
*Endymion*:

> cold springs had run
> To warm their chilliest bubbles in the grass,[2]

or to his description of the 'hurrying freshnesses' in 'I stood
tiptoe upon a little hill', with the swarms of minnows

> Staying their wavy bodies 'gainst the streams,
> To taste the luxury of sunny beams
> Temper'd with coolness.[3]

Sometimes Cowper, too, will enter in this way into the very
nature of the being or object contemplated, but at other times
he is content to stand outside or apart from it, and to describe
it (or, more accurately, allude to it) in the conventional terms
of his poetic diction.

The pagan deities constituted a notable part of this diction.[4]
In fairness to the poets we must recognize that they were a
genuine part of the eighteenth-century scene, and that they
were very far from being confined to poetry. They appeared
frequently in the paintings of Reynolds and his contemporaries,
they stood or reclined upon the outside of public buildings and

---

[1] *The Task*, i. 236 ff.          [2] i. 102 f.
[3] ll. 73 ff.                         [4] See Note N, p. 171.

filled niches in the interior, they wriggled their way into chairs
and tables and beds, they warmed themselves on fire-places,
they hunted or caroused on tapestries and urns and screens,
and to the dismay of some Christians they even penetrated into
the parish church in the more elaborate monuments erected
to ladies and gentlemen deceased. A writer in the *Connoisseur*
(25 March 1756) speculates facetiously on the revenue which
might be raised by a tax on heathen gods in the gardens of the
great: the nobleman at his seat, the esquire at the hall-house,
the citizen in his country-box, and even the divine at his
parsonage, all have their walks and gardens peopled with
satyrs, fauns, and dryads.

While infidelity has expunged the Christian theology from our creed,
taste has introduced the heathen mythology into our gardens. If a
pond is dug, Neptune, at the command of taste, emerges from the
bason, and presides in the middle; or if a vista is cut through a grove,
it must be terminated by a Flora, or an Apollo.

If the pagan gods had not become fully naturalized in eighteenth-
century England, they entered much more fully into the consciousness of the educated Englishman than they do to-day.
He first met them as a schoolboy in Ovid and Virgil and in the
copperplates of Tooke's *Pantheon*,[1] and he was continually
reminded of them in later life as a part of his cultural heritage.

But repetition (as Keats feared unnecessarily for his own
*Endymion*) had 'dulled their brightness'. Even in the reign of
Queen Anne there were voices protesting against the too frequent introduction of Greek deities into English poetry. As
the years passed, and Apollo and Diana, Boreas and Aeolus, the
Nymphs and the Dryads were still brought in to brighten the
page, the old heathen mythology became more and more mori-
bund. Johnson let slip no opportunity of condemning what he
had come to regard as a boring and lifeless convention. 'The
attention', he once observed, 'naturally retires from a new tale
of Venus, Diana, and Minerva';[2] and of the second stanza in
'The Progress of Poesy' he remarked crossly: 'Criticism disdains
to chase a schoolboy to his common-places.'[3] Only a few years
after Johnson's death, another sturdy and intelligent Englishman was showing no mercy to the schoolboys at Christ's Hos-

---

[1] The remarkable popularity of this work tells its own tale. First published in
1698, it had reached a thirty-fifth edition by 1824.
[2] *Lives*, ii. 283 (of Gay's *The Fan*).                    [3] Ibid. iii. 436.

pital (young Coleridge among them) when they thought to embellish their English compositions with classical clichés and pagan deities:

Lute, harp, and lyre, Muse, Muses, and inspirations, Pegasus, Parnassus, and Hippocrene were all abominations to him. In fancy I can almost hear him now, exclaiming 'Harp? Harp? Lyre? Pen and ink, boy, you mean! Muse, boy, Muse? Your nurse's daughter, you mean! Pierian spring? Oh aye! the cloister-pump, I suppose!'[1]

A more reasoned objection to the continual use of classical mythology in modern English poetry was made by Henry Mackenzie in 1785. What was natural (he argues) to the Greeks, and indeed an essential part of their religious system, is no longer natural to us. Thus far, Mackenzie is only repeating the argument of Johnson and of the many others who had by this time come round to Johnson's point of view. But he has a further objection to offer.

Another bad consequence of this servile imitation of the ancients . . . has been to prevent modern authors from studying nature as it is, from attempting to draw it as it really appears; and, instead of giving genuine descriptions, it leads them to give those only which are false and artificial.[2]

In fact, Flora, Zephyrus, Pan, Pomona, Aurora, and the rest had become poetical contractions for something that ought to have been described at full length; and not being under the necessity of so describing it, the poet (Mackenzie suggests) had ended by not really seeing it at all. Which is the effect here and which the cause it would be hard to say. Did poets write

Here blushing Flora paints the enamelled ground

because they had failed to see what lay before their eyes, or did blushing Flora prevent them from seeing by removing the occasion for observation? Certainly if every stream is to be a Naiad it will be difficult to differentiate one stream from another. But here we are thrown back again on eighteenth-century theory, which held that the poet is to paint not the particular but the general. When, in course of time, the desire to particularize grew more and more insistent, and we find Wordsworth spending several stanzas in describing an aged thorn which he had observed on the ridge of Quantock Hill on

[1] *Biographia Literaria*, i. 5.
[2] *The Lounger*, No. 37, 10 Oct. 1785.

a stormy day, and putting his description into the mouth of 'a
captain of a small trading vessel . . ., who being past the middle
age of life, had retired upon an annuity or small independent
income to some village or country town of which he was not a
native, or in which he had not been accustomed to live',[1] then,
not unnaturally, the old gods must go with the kind of poetry
that made their continuing existence possible.

## VI

It will be recalled that Johnson defended Pope's poetic
diction in the *Homer* not only on the ground that the demand
for elegance had increased in those more sophisticated modern
days, but also on the ground that 'knowledge finds no willing
reception [nowadays] till it be recommended by artificial
diction'.[2] It was an idea to which he often recurred. The value
of poetic diction lay partly in its power to make the reader pay
attention to what he might otherwise neglect. In discussing
Swift's prose he had noted how clearly and easily Swift always
conveyed his meaning.

For purposes merely didactick [he continues] when something is to
be told that was not known before, it is the best mode, but against
that inattention by which known truths are suffered to lie neglected
it makes no provision; it instructs, but does not persuade.[3]

Eighteenth-century poetry was only too full of those known
truths; indeed, as we have seen, no other sort of truth was
willingly admitted. If, therefore, the known truths were to
attract attention, it must be as ladies and gentlemen would
attract attention at a ball or an assembly—by the richness and
elegance of their dress. Vicesimus Knox, who often followed
in the path of Johnson like a literary jackal, reached the same
conclusion in an essay 'On the Expediency of embellishing
Composition with Harmonious Periods, and with other judicious Ornaments . Modern writers, he tells us, 'find it difficult
to add novelty to the matter, because, in the course of a few
ages, every subject is frequently treated, and consequently soon
exhausted'. But a modern writer who cannot hope to add anything new to the philosophy of a Bacon or a Newton 'may yet
deliver their thoughts in such a manner, and refine their

---

[1] *The Poetical Works of William Wordsworth*, ed. E. De Selincourt, ii. 512.
[2] Cf. p. 140.                                    [3] *Lives*, ii. 52.

beauties with such ornaments of diction' that his work may be more widely read than that of the original author. In a later passage he compares writing with building, and draws a distinction between that sort of building which merely answers the purpose of providing shelter, and that which also delights and surprises because 'the chisel in the master's hand' has 'called forth each latent beauty, added the festoon and the Corinthian foliage'.[1] Here the conception of poetic diction as a sort of decorative effect on the plain surface of the idea is fully established. Some such notion must have been in the mind of John Gwynn the architect when he engaged in argument with Johnson as they shared a coach on the way to Oxford. Johnson had been talking against ornament in architecture; Gwynn offered to defend it.

'What, Sir, will you allow no value to beauty in architecture or in statuary? Why should we allow it then in writing? Why do you take the trouble to give us so many fine allusions, and bright images, and elegant phrases? You might convey all your instructions without these ornaments.' Johnson smiled with complacency; but said, 'Why, Sir, all these ornaments are useful, because they obtain an easier reception for truth; but a building is not at all more convenient for being decorated with superfluous carved work.'[2]

In Johnson's reply we can see again his concern for the *memorable* conveyance of known truths. The poet, no less than the prose-writer, had to struggle constantly to defeat the inattention of his readers. He, too, could use fine allusions and bright images, but poetic diction was his most reliable weapon. In the end it was to defeat the poet's intentions. The weapon, once so sharp and new, had become blunted by constant use, and the inattention of readers was no longer to be startled by a poetic diction that had acquired almost the sanctity of the Church service. When that day came, something very different was required if readers were still to be startled—nothing less, indeed, than 'the language really spoken by men'. The shock administered by Wordsworth is itself an indication of how much it was needed.

[1] *Essays, Moral and Literary* (1821 ed.), i. 251 f., 254.
[2] Boswell, *Life*, ii. 439.

# IX

# TRUANTS AND REBELS

I

IT would have been surprising if the type of poetry that came
in with *Cooper's Hill* (1642) and was firmly established by
1680 had satisfied all the poets and their readers for the next
hundred and fifty years. There were some whom it failed to
satisfy completely, and towards the end of the eighteenth century some whom it did not please at all. But over the greater
part of the period there was a quite remarkable unanimity about
what poetry was and how it should be written; and even those
who were willing to escape from some of the restrictions imposed
on the poets by current literary theory often made their escape
in a disciplined manner, and even used their liberty to set up
new rules and regulations.

There were, in fact, a number of well-recognized ways of
taking a holiday from the Rules, and of escaping from the prevailing atmosphere of good sense into a rarer and more volatile
air. So long as you made it clear that you were going *deliberately* beyond the normal range of eighteenth-century thought
and feeling, or alternatively made no pretence to be writing
quite seriously, you might ignore most of the foundations on
which contemporary poetry was so solidly based—Nature,
Good Sense, Correctness, Elegance, and much else.

A favourite excursion into wilder regions than were normally
visited at this period was by way of the Pindaric ode. Cowley
had established the English attitude to Pindar: 'If a man
should undertake to translate Pindar word for word, it would
be thought that one madman had translated another. . . .'[1]
Congreve, it is true, objected to the notion that the Pindaric
ōde was merely wild and irregular,[2] and some later critics em-
phasized the method in Pindar's madness. Yet most English
imitators of Pindar felt free, if not to be mad, at least to write
in a much wilder fashion than would normally have been
acceptable. Giles Jacob, whose evidence is valuable here
because he is so completely devoid of any ideas of his own,
informed the readers of one of the most popular contemporary

---

[1] Chalmers, vii. 125.  [2] Ibid. x. 301.

guide-books to poetry that the Pindaric ode 'allows (in the English language) more latitude than any other poem'.[1]

So apparently thought Pomfret. His best-known poem, 'The Choice', is a perfect embodiment of the reasonable attitude to life; the poet moves contentedly among the things of every day, making no extravagant demands of fortune but indulging his fancy in temperate Horatian delights. Pomfret, however, also wrote several Pindaric odes. In two of those especially, 'On the General Conflagration and Ensuing Judgment' and 'Dies Novissima', he lets his imagination bolt with his reason, and even (one sometimes feels) sits watching it from the grand stand and cheers it on. How else are we to account for this vision of the Last Day?

> Reverse all Nature's web shall run,
>    And spotless Misrule all around,
>    Order, its flying foe, confound;
> Whilst backward all the threads shall haste to be unspun.
>    Triumphant Chaos, with his oblique wand,
> (The wand with which, ere time begun,
>    His wandering slaves he did command,
> And made them scamper right, and in rude ranges run)
>    The hostile Harmony shall chase;
> And as the Nymph resigns her place,
>    And, panting, to the neighbouring refuge flies,
>    The formless ruffian slaughters with his eyes,
>    And, following, storms the perching dame's retreat,
>    Adding the terrors of his threat;
> The globe shall faintly tremble round,
> And backward jolt, distorted with the wound.
>
> Swath'd in substantial shrouds of night,
> The sickening Sun shall from the world retire,
>    Stripp'd of his dazzling robes of fire;
> Which, dangling, once shed round a lavish flood of light!
>    No frail eclipse, but all essential shade,
>    Not yielding to primeval gloom,
>    Whilst day was yet an embryo in the womb;
> Nor glimmering in its source, with silver streamers play'd,
> A jetty mixture of the darkness spread
>    O'er murmuring Egypt's head;
>    And that which angels drew
> O'er Nature's face, when Jesus died;

[1] *An Historical Account of the Lives and Writings of the Most Eminent English Poets* (2nd ed.), 1733, p. xxiii.

Which sleeping ghosts for this mistook,
And, rising, off their hanging funerals shook,
And fleeting pass'd, expos'd their bloodless breast to view,
   Yet find it not so dark, and to their dormitories glide.[1]

Pomfret can write like this because he is a poet (though here he
is going rather beyond his powers), and because he is a priest of
the Church of England whose imagination has been nurtured
by the Book of Revelation; he knows that he *may* write like this
because he is writing a Pindaric ode. So, too, Isaac Watts,
similarly inspired and writing in the Pindaric form, has often a
freedom of movement and an imaginative energy that mark
him out as a Dissenter in poetry as well as in religion. How he
thought of the Pindaric ode emerges clearly from the opening
stanza of one of his own pindarics:

Wild as the lightning, various as the Moon,
   Roves my Pindaric song:
Here she glows like burning noon
In fiercest flames, and here she plays
Gentle as star-beams on the midnight seas;
   Now in a smiling angel's form,
   Anon she rides upon the storm,
Loud as the noisy thunder, as a deluge strong.
   Are my thoughts and wishes free,
   And know no number nor degree?
Such is the Muse: Lo she disdains
   The links and chains,
   Measures and rules of vulgar strains,
And o'er the laws of harmony a sovereign queen she reigns.[2]

It is not merely a mingled measure that Watts is allowing himself: even more significant (if we are thinking of his departure
from the normal practice of his day) are the mingling of moods,
the transition within one poem from the fierce to the gentle,
the variegated emotional tone.

Perhaps the clearest statement of the sort of licence that
could safely be claimed by the writer of odes is that offered to
the readers of Young's 'Ocean: an Ode' (1728). The Ode,
Young insists, should be

rapturous, somewhat abrupt, and immethodical to a vulgar eye.
That apparent order, and connexion, which gives form and life to

---

[1] Chalmers, viii. 335 f. ('Dies Novissima').
[2] Ibid., xiii. 41 ('Two Happy Rivals').

*some* compositions, takes away the very soul of *this*. . . . It is the genuine character, and true merit of the ode, a little to startle some apprehensions. Men of cold complexions are very apt to mistake a want of vigour in their imaginations, for a delicacy of taste in their judgements; and, like persons of a tender sight, they look on bright objects, in their natural lustre, as too glaring; what is most delightful to a stronger eye, is painful to them. Thus Pindar, who has as much logic at the bottom as Aristotle or Euclid, to some critics has appeared as mad; and must appear so to all who enjoy no portion of his own divine spirit. Dwarf-understandings, measuring others by their own standard, are apt to think they see a monster, when they see a man.[1]

Judgement, he continues, 'that masculine power of the mind, in ode, as in all compositions, should bear the supreme sway'; it should still, even in the ode, control the imagination.

But then in ode, there is this difference from other kinds of poetry; that, there, the imagination, like a very beautiful mistress, is indulged in the appearance of domineering; though the judgment, like an artful lover, in reality carries its point; and the less it is suspected of it, it shows the more masterly conduct, and deserves the greater commendation.

It holds true in this province of writing, as in war, 'The more danger, the more honour'. It must be very enterprising; it must, in Shakespeare's style, have hair-breadth 'scapes; and often tread the very brink of errour: nor can it ever deserve the applause of the *real* judge, unless it renders itself obnoxious to the misapprehensions of the contrary.[2]

Young's critical insight here was stronger than his creative power: the ode to which those remarks were prefaced is more in Ercles' than in Pindar's vein. In his *Night Thoughts*, too, Young's willingness to have 'hair-breadth 'scapes' often led to a vague and grandiose utterance which suggests sublimity rather than achieves it. Yet he saw more clearly than most that there was another mode of thought than that 'order and connexion' which gave life and form to so much eighteenth-century poetry; there was, in fact, an order that was apparently fortuitous and unmethodical, but that had a rapturous and abrupt method of its own. So far, so good; but even as Young is pleading so eloquently for freedom we can perhaps see the Pindaric ode freezing into the rigidity of another 'kind', with a calculated and required abruptness and a methodical want of method. So

[1] Ibid., p. 403.  [2] Ibid., p. 404.

Ambrose Philips, in some verses addressed to William Pulteney (1723), manages to suggest that the Ode is at once perfectly free and perfectly restrained:

> What laws shall o'er the Ode preside?
> In vain would Art presume to guide
> The chariot-wheels of praise,
> When Fancy, driving, ranges free,
> Fresh flowers selecting, like the bee,
> And *regularly strays*.[1]

The Ode, at any rate, continued throughout the century to supply a means of escape from neo-classical orthodoxy. Whether it proved to be popular reading or not, it was certainly popular with the poets themselves; and if odes were often undertaken by some of the feeblest writers of the period in the mistaken belief that they were easy to write, the Ode also provided such poets as Collins and Gray with a mode of lyrical utterance that the eighteenth century was prepared to accept. But the acceptance was governed by the understanding that the ode—and, above all, the Pindaric ode—was a special case, and that the main stream of poetry was altogether less turbulent. Though Pindar must be accounted sane, that sort of abruptness and apparent inconsequence which characterized the Pindaric ode was normally associated in the eighteenth-century mind with madness. When a character goes mad in an eighteenth-century play the usual signs of the disorder are a complete absence of logical connexion in the sequence of ideas. It is in this fashion that Sheridan's Tilburina runs mad in *The Critic*:[2]

> The wind whistles—the moon rises—see,
> They have kill'd my squirrel in his cage: . . .
> An oyster may be cross'd in love! Who says
> A whale's a bird?

Right to the end of the century the prestige of reason remained high; and reason demanded that even the poet should not proceed in too irrational fashion. As his eye travelled with pleasure over the regular and expected elevations of an eighteenth-century building, so the mind of the contemporary reader counted on finding a controlled and continuous argument in a poem. He did not object to feeling or fancy in due measure, but he looked first for good sense; the blinding visions

---

[1] Chalmers, xiii. 123.          [2] III. i.

of a Smart or a Blake were little more to him than 'exhalations whizzing in the air'.

## II

Pindar was a venerable name, an Ancient, and his authority could be used to justify a good deal in his modern imitators. To a somewhat slighter extent the English Ancients—Spenser, Shakespeare, Milton—could obtain a hearing for a modern poet who wished to go outside the normal range of poetic subject and poetic diction. Nicholas Rowe and one or two others wrote plays in imitation of Shakespeare's style; but the eighteenth century was so firmly convinced that Shakespeare's style was the worst thing about him that the attempts were not numerous and were never carried very far. Imitations of Spenser and Milton, however, were frequent. A late eighteenth-century collection of English poetry gives two of its eighteen volumes to imitations of Spenser and Milton, and this roughly indicates the importance of such poems in the period. The words 'Written in Imitation of Spenser's Style' at the head of a poem served to disarm criticism, except that grumbling kind of criticism that said it was foolish to imitate Spenser at all. They were an indication to the reader that the poem should not be—or, at any rate, need not be—taken very seriously; but if you chose to take it seriously, so much the better. It was in this spirit that Shenstone wrote 'The Schoolmistress'. To Lady Luxborough in 1748 he confided his intentions: 'I meant to skreen the ridicule which might fall on so *low* a subject (tho' perhaps a *picturesque* one) by *pretending* to *simper* all the time I was writing.'[1] The poet's reputation was not at stake, as it would have been if he had written in one of the recognized Kinds and in the contemporary poetic idiom. Such, no doubt, was the theory. In practice, the Spenserian stanza was a sort of fancy dress in which the modern poet could behave with a poetical freedom that he would not have ventured upon in his own conventional clothes. Though some of the imitations are merely ludicrous in purpose and performance, most of the poets who attempted to imitate Spenser fell under the influence of his leisurely rhythm and wrote more seriously than they may have intended; and one or two of them, like the author of *The Castle of Indolence*, caught something of Spenser's sleepy music,

[1] *The Letters of William Shenstone*, ed. Marjorie Williams, 1939, p. 145.

so remote from the characteristic rhythms of the wide-awake
and dialectical eighteenth century. Equally important was the
influence on the eighteenth-century poet of Spenser's richness
and colour and his shimmering world of knights and fair ladies,
ogres and dragons, green valleys and flowery meadows. On the
mind of the eighteenth-century reader, accustomed to the cold
unbroken light of reason, Spenser's poetry must have had
something of the effect of a stained-glass window. You might
prefer clear Georgian windows for your living-rooms, but you
might enjoy (as Pope enjoyed at Stanton Harcourt) the colour
and quaintness of an earlier age. The conscious imitation of
Spenser, therefore, gave the eighteenth-century poet a change
of air, a change of mood; it provided him with a pleasant way
of slipping off his responsibilities, and allowed him to return
undisgraced and unspoilt to his proper business of writing contemporary poetry for contemporary readers.

Milton, or, at any rate, Miltonic blank verse proved useful to
the writers of georgic and descriptive verse, where they would
have found the heroic couplet less well suited to their purpose.
The numerous imitations of *L'Allegro* and *Il Penseroso* in the
middle years of the eighteenth century point rather to the need
of finding expression for a new kind of mood than to the mere
following of a literary fashion. But it is in the high contemporary reputation of such poems as *The Splendid Shilling* (1705)
and *Cyder* (1708) that we can find the main influence of Milton
on the new century. To John Philips Milton was clearly a
great lord of language: the admiration that was grudgingly
withheld from Shakespeare (who wrote 'in the style of a bad
age') was generously lavished in the eighteenth century on
the sounding utterance of Milton. In Philips's burlesque of
Milton's verse we have a startling example of how 'each man
kills the thing he loves'. To imitate Milton as well as Philips
sometimes does, a parodist must both understand and admire
his author; to burlesque Milton *at such length* as Philips does
he must have a curious want of confidence in himself or in his
readers. Almost any poet in his lighter moments might parody
the work of his predecessors; the significant thing about Philips
is that he never does anything else. The mood remains half-
serious; Philips makes sure that you won't laugh at him because he has laughed first. The 'annual jollities' of the rustics
at Christmas time are so described:

Now sportive youth
Carol incondite rhythms, with suiting notes,
And quaver unharmonious; sturdy swains
In clean array, for rustic dance prepare,
Mixt with the buxom damsels; hand in hand
They frisk, and bound, and various mazes weave,
Shaking their brawny limbs, with uncouth mein,
Transported, and sometimes, an oblique leer
Dart on their loves, sometimes, an hasty kiss
Steal from unwary lasses; they with scorn,
And neck reclin'd, resent the ravish'd bliss.
Mean while, blind British bards with volant touch
Traverse loquacious strings, whose solemn notes
Provoke to harmless revels; these among,
A subtle artist stands, in wondrous bag
That bears imprison'd winds, (of gentler sort
Than those which erst Laertes' son enclos'd) . . . .[1]

The burlesque in Philips varies from the ribald to the refined,
but it is never long absent; sometimes he almost seems to forget
it and to revel in the polysyllabic harmonies of Milton, but
once again he 'darts an oblique leer' at his author, and the
spell is broken. Before long, however, Milton was to be taken
much more seriously, and his generous rhythms and large
periods did much to free eighteenth-century poetry from those
intellectual 'points and turns' which the heroic couplet had too
exclusively induced. With the passage from Philips we may
compare another description of rural jollities from Thomson:

Rustic mirth goes round—
The simple joke that takes the shepherd's heart,
Easily pleased; the long loud laugh sincere;
The kiss, snatched hasty from the sidelong maid
On purpose guardless, or pretending sleep;
The leap, the slap, the haul; and shook to notes
Of native music, the respondent dance.
Thus jocund fleets with them the winter-night.[2]

The whole tone, of course, is different; the rustics are no longer
figures of fun for a scholar; they stand at least half-way between
'the labourer ox' or 'the bleating kind' and the Right Hon.
Sir Spencer Compton, to whom the poem is addressed. But the
voice—though much more faintly—is still the voice of Milton,

[1] *Cyder*, ii. 413 ff. (Chalmers, viii. 394).
[2] *The Seasons* ('Winter', ll. 622 ff.).

and the faintness of the imitation is in direct ratio to the greater seriousness of the poet's intention. Thomson has far too much to say to be merely an imitator; in so far as he imitates Milton he does so because Milton helps him to express, in a way that the eighteenth century will accept, what he wants to say. Philips, on the other hand, is typical of the century's interest in style for its own sake. *The Splendid Shilling* is primarily an exercise in poetic diction, and also, of course, in the mock-heroic.[1]

### III

The popularity of mock-heroic in the eighteenth century is a literary phenomenon of real significance. An essential condition of this popularity was a much greater familiarity with the Heroic (or Epic) which was being mocked than is generally found among twentieth-century readers.[2] In some ways the reputation of this genre is a disquieting sign; it seems to point to a public which can respond contentedly to what has the sound of poetry without the substance, a public that likes to have its knowledge flattered by being invited to recall what (of Homer, Virgil, Milton) it already knows. But the mock-heroic must also have supplied the eighteenth-century reader with something that was too often missing from the more serious poetry of the age. It involved a comical reversal of literary standards; the poet was laughing at the pedantry and rigidity of the Rules, poking the critics in the ribs, mocking recklessly at his own too habitual solemnities. Carried along on a wave of high spirits, he could, and often did, revel in fantasy and absurdity, in grotesque exaggeration and wild caricature. And he called upon his readers for a more flexible and even imaginative response than was normally required of them. Classical art, for all its virtues, is marked by a certain rigidity, a preference for one thing at a time, an unwillingness to entertain conflicting elements of thought, feeling, and experience; it rejects the mixed effect, and aims always at unity of tone. With a Wren church or a Georgian dwelling-house everything is of a piece, everything makes in the same direction; and the mind takes in the unified effect, not necessarily at a glance, but in a series of related impressions, each new impression reinforcing all those that have preceded it. The same can be said of such character-

---

[1] See Note O, p. 171.  [2] Cf. pp. 55 ff.

istically classical poems as Gray's *Elegy*, which holds gravely
and steadily on its way, maintaining throughout the same
measured pace and the same solemn tone. Classical art, then,
avoids what it cannot reduce to its own habitual order and
proportion; it normally declines to attempt what Coleridge
considered to be one of the cardinal achievements of the poet,
'the balance or reconciliation of opposite or discordant qualities'.
The classical and neo-classical quarrel with tragi-comedy is
only one of the most familiar expressions of this dislike of the
heterogeneous; it appears again in a distaste for the Gothic
cathedral with its saints and its gargoyles and its bewildering
complexity, for the medieval drama with its reverence and
ribaldry, its tears and laughter, for Metaphysical poetry with
its incalculable transitions from one mood or one thought to
another. But here in the mock-heroic poetry of the eighteenth
century we do find something of this mixed effect. To appreciate it fully a reader had to hover expectantly between two
levels of response; he had to be aware all the time of the heroic,
or else he could not enjoy the mockery. Mock-heroic poetry,
in fact, set up literary vibrations that demanded from him a
special sort of divided awareness.

That the eighteenth-century reader did not always manage
to respond adequately may be seen from the ludicrous complaint of John Dennis that the action of the *Dunciad* was full of
improbabilities:

But what probability is there in Pope's rhapsody? What probability
in the games which take up a third part of the piece? Is it not monstrous to imagine any thing like that in the master street of a popu-
lous city; a street eternally crowded with carriages, carts, coaches,
chairs, and men passing in the greatest hurry about private and
publick affairs?[1]

What are we to make of this? It is true that Dennis was doing
his best to think up objections to Pope's poem; but what is to
be said of a reader who objects to the mock-heroic because it is
improbable? Dennis's hatred of puns must have been only one
aspect of a deadly seriousness that made him cling tenaciously
to the actual and the probable, and repudiate not only fun and
fantasy, but anything that was not literally true. To escape
from such readers was indeed to find freedom.

[1] *Critical Works*, ii. 362.

The comic reversal of values in which the mock-heroic indulged, its magnifying of trifles, its flippant exaggerations, are, in fact, the characteristic fantasy of the aristocratic mind. In the plays of Congreve we often meet with a delicately comic fantasy which is the very poetry of artificiality and affectation. We recognize the authentic note in the dialogue between Millamant and Mincing on the subject of love-letters:

*Mrs. Millamant.* O ay, letters—I had letters—I am persecuted with letters—I hate letters—Nobody knows how to write letters, and yet one has 'em, one does not know why. They serve to pin up one's hair.

*Witwoud.* Is that the way? Pray, madam, do you pin up your hair with all your letters? I find I must keep copies.

*Mrs. Mil.* Only with those in verse, Mr. Witwoud; I never pin my hair up with prose.—I think I tried once, Mincing.

*Mincing.* O mem, I shall never forget it.

*Mrs. Mil.* Ay, poor Mincing tift and tift all the morning.

*Mincing.* Till I had the cramp in my fingers, I'll vow, mem: and all to no purpose. But when your la'-ship pins it up with poetry, it sits so pleasant the next day as anything, and is so pure and so *crips*.[1]

From such exquisite affectations—the fanciful triflings of the polite, bored by their own correctness and yet correct even in their mocking protest—it is only a little step to the fantasy of Pope:

> For this, ere Phoebus rose, he had implor'd
> Propitious Heav'n, and ev'ry pow'r ador'd,
> But chiefly love—to love an altar built,
> Of twelve vast French romances, neatly gilt.
> There lay three garters, half a pair of gloves;
> And all the trophies of his former loves.
> With tender billet-doux he lights the pyre,
> And breathes three am'rous sighs to raise the fire. . . .[2]

or,

> To fifty chosen sylphs, of special note,
> We trust th' important charge, the petticoat:
> Oft have we known that sev'nfold fence to fail,
> Tho' stiff with hoops, and arm'd with ribs of whale.
> Form a strong line about the silver bound,
> And guard the wide circumference around.[3]

[1] *The Way of the World*, ii. ii.    [2] *The Rape of the Lock*, ii. 35 ff.
[3] Ibid. ii. 117 ff.

In such lovely absurdities as those the eighteenth-century poet at once satisfied the standards of polite taste and escaped into a freer and more exquisite world, where only the intelligent and the sensitive (and, once more, the well educated) could follow him.

The freedom conferred upon the poet by the mock-heroic enabled him to ignore or modify normal eighteenth-century practice at various other points. His descriptive passages, for example, were often more detailed and individualized than was common in the more serious poetry of the age. That the poets were willing enough, when they found an excuse, to forget all about 'general properties and large appearances' may be seen from the description of the toilet table in *The Rape of the Lock*, where Pope is busy numbering the streaks in Belinda's combs. Gay, too, can safely paint with almost Hogarthian detail a winter scene in the London streets:

> On silent wheel the passing coaches roll;
> Oft' look behind, and ward the threatening pole.
> In harden'd orbs the school-boy moulds the snow,
> To mark the coachman with a dext'rous throw.
> Why do ye, boys, the kennel's surface spread,
> To tempt with faithless pass the matron's tread?
> How can ye laugh to see the damsel spurn,
> Sink in your frauds, and her green stockings mourn?
> At White's the harness'd chairman idly stands,
> And swings around his waist his tingling hands:
> The sempstress speeds to 'Change with red-tipt nose;
> The Belgian stove beneath her footstool glows;
> In half-whipt muslin needles useless lie,
> And shuttle-cocks across the counter fly.[1]

Or again, in *The Shepherd's Week*, he can touch delicately on the details of Blouzelinda's butter-making:

> Sometimes, like wax, she rolls the butter round,
> Or with the wooden lilly prints the pound.[2]

Mock-heroic, and still more burlesque, also permitted and even encouraged the grotesque. Examples abound in the *Dunciad*; the most memorable is perhaps the diving-match in Book II, where Smedley takes the horrible plunge into Fleet-ditch—

> slow circles dimpled o'er
> The quaking mud, that clos'd, and ope'd no more—

---

[1] *Trivia*, ii. 327 ff. (Chalmers, x. 459).     [2] 'Friday', ll. 59 f. (ibid., p. 451).

only to reappear again with dramatic suddenness after his short sojourn among the mud-nymphs:

> Sudden, a burst of thunder shook the flood.
> Lo Smedley rose, in majesty of mud!
> Shaking the horrors of his ample brows,
> And each ferocious feature grim with ooze. . . .[1]

The passage recalls Gay's equally grotesque vision of Cloacina rising from the same obscene waters:

> While thus he fervent prays, the heaving tide
> In widen'd circles beats on either side;
> The goddess rose amidst the inmost round,
> With wither'd turnip tops her temples crown'd;
> Low reach'd her dripping tresses, lank and black
> As the smooth jet, or glossy raven's back;
> Around her waist a circling eel was twin'd,
> Which bound her robe that hung in rags behind.[2]

Gay wrote for the polite, for the man of culture, and the lady of fashion. How, it may be asked, do such grotesque images find their way into the poetry of a polite society? It has already been suggested that this polite society was precariously balanced between a highly artificial formality and a constantly encroaching vulgarity. But neither Pope nor Gay has slithered unintentionally on the garbage that lay about the Augustan streets. In such grotesqueries polite society is escaping from its own negative perfections. Correctness has become a burden, restraint has become intolerable; and the eighteenth-century poet, like a schoolboy breaking away from his desk at the end of the hour, covers himself happily with mud in the playing-field. Nature driven out with a pitchfork has found her way back in a refuse-cart.

## IV

Literary historians are entitled to define eighteenth-century poetry or 'the poetry of the Augustan age' in their own terms, but they sometimes write about it as if it was commensurate with the poetry of Pope alone. This may be an unintentional tribute to Pope's contemporary importance; yet there is surely something wrong with a definition that leaves out most of the other notable poets of the age—Thomson, Gray, Collins, Gold-

---

[1] *The Dunciad* (1729), ii. 279 f., 301 ff.
[2] *Trivia*, ii. 193 ff. (Chalmers, x. 458).

smith, Cowper, Crabbe—on the grounds that they were in
revolt from its poetical standards, and groping their way with
varying success towards the dawn of romanticism. Thomson
may have been impatient with that sort of verse which consists
of little more than neatly turned thoughts (what Lord Fopping-
ton called 'the forced sprauts' of a man's brain), Dyer may have
been attracted by ruins and Gray by churchyards and mountains, Collins may have shown an interest in popular superstitions and Goldsmith in a deserted village, without repudiating
or even expressing much dissatisfaction with the culture of
their own day. Such poets widened the range of eighteenth-
century sensibility, but they accepted without much protest the
contemporary poetic idiom and continued to work contentedly
within the tradition.

Yet there were some who did wish to overthrow and to
destroy. Unorthodox, because consciously in revolt, were such
men as Joseph and Thomas Warton. When we find Joseph
Warton expressing a desire to go with silent footsteps

> To charnels and the house of woe,
> To Gothic churches, vaults, and tombs,
> Where each sad night some virgin comes,
> With throbbing breast, and faded cheek,
> Her promised bridegroom's urn to seek . . .[1]

we may not approve the wish, or feel called upon to admire the
poetry, but we are bound to recognize a conscious flight from
the sensible and sociable pleasures of the eighteenth century
to something morbid and much more emotional. When we
hear his brother Thomas (at the age of seventeen) asking
Melancholy to lead him

> to solemn glooms
> Congenial with my soul; to cheerless shades,
> To ruin'd seats, to twilight cells and bow'rs,

where all is silent

> Save the lone screech-owl's note, who builds his bow'r
> Amid the mould'ring caverns dark and damp,[2]

we may attribute the lines to the natural morbidity of the
adolescent, but we are in the presence of a sensibility which, if
it spreads, will change the face of English poetry.

[1] 'Ode to Fancy' (Chalmers, xviii. 164).
[2] 'The Pleasures of Melancholy' (ibid., p. 95).

What the Wartons were trying, not always successfully, to do in their verse, they reinforced with their more influential criticism. So, too, Young challenged the neo-classical standards in his *Night Thoughts* (1742–5), and, more deliberately, in his *Conjectures on Original Composition* (1759). The *Night Thoughts*, formless, egotistical, vague, unrestrained, ambitious, and grandiose, continually promising rather more than they are able to perform, are the antithesis of almost all that neo-classical poetry stands for; and yet they were enormously popular. Young, with his bleeding heart, his secret or his suggestion of a secret, his determined gloom, his conscious loneliness, is an early romantic egoist, a Byron of the middle classes, whose woes, real or imaginary, fell with an impressive sound on the ears of a listening Europe.

Forty years later, in *The Task*, Cowper has passed beyond Young's conscious self-display to the almost unconscious self-revelation that we meet with so often in Romantic poetry. Cowper writes easily and confidingly about himself, expecting the reader (if, indeed, he considers the matter at all) to be interested. Pope, it is true, had written about himself in the *Epistle to Dr. Arbuthnot*; but it was for the most part about his public self as a man of letters who had been attacked and vilified for a quarter of a century. So, too, the 'Verses on the Death of Dr. Swift' presuppose a literary public to whom Swift has grown familiar, and there is no self-revelation. But such passages as Cowper's 'I was a stricken deer that left the herd'[1] have the character of confessions; the poet is laying bare his inmost experience. Perhaps we see the change that is coming over poetry even more startlingly in those passages where Cowper recalls some triviality in his private life which can have little significance for anyone but himself and his immediate circle of friends:

> Once went I forth, and found, till then unknown,
> A cottage, whither oft we since repair:
> 'Tis perched upon the green hill top, but close
> Environed with a ring of branching elms
> That overhang the thatch, itself unseen
> Peeps at the vale below; so thick beset
> With foliage of such dark redundant growth,
> I called the low-roofed lodge the Peasant's Nest.[2]

---

[1] *The Task*, iii. 108.     [2] Ibid. i. 220 ff.

What of it? we are apt to exclaim. Why should you expect that those private and particular reminiscences will interest us? Here, as in several other respects, Cowper oddly anticipates Wordsworth, whose 'Poems on the Naming of Places' impart to us, along with much that is fine, some purely domestic recollections and sentiments that we could well spare. If Pope had named an echoing crag 'Joanna's (or Patty's or Tessie's) Peak' he would have kept the fact to himself and his own immediate friends; but to the Romantic poet the whole world is his confessional. 'This happens to all men,' says the classical poet; 'it must therefore be important.' The Romantic poet, always prone to argue from his own personal experience, is more apt to say: 'This was important to *me*; it must therefore be so to all men.'

Even more remarkable, perhaps, as an indication of changing tastes was the success of James Macpherson's 'Ossian' poems (1760–3). Melancholy, which earlier in the century had been not much more than a fashionable disorder—the spleen, or the low-spirited 'leucocholy' mentioned by Gray in one of his early letters—here reached a sombre magnificence that seemed to be its own justification. Vague, infinitely sad, full of regret for vanished splendours, wild and exclamatory, mysterious, visionary, Macpherson's *Fragments* owed their success not so much to a genuine emotion as to a spurious emotionalism, to a willing suspension of good sense and a significant preference for the undefined and imprecise. The reader who abandons himself to Macpherson is willing to wander among dim shapes and bare landscapes that are periodically blotted out by mists; he is drugged, too, by a rhythm which is at once exciting and monotonous. Suggestion here has become more important than statement.

In some of the poetry of Christopher Smart, and in almost all that Blake wrote, the eighteenth-century tradition received another sort of shock, perhaps the most serious of all. The poetry written in England from the time of Dryden had been in the main a poetry of measured statement and discourse. The poetry of Dryden, Pope, Thomson, Johnson, Gray, Goldsmith is not *merely* a poetry of good sense, but good sense it is. The poetical structure is not held together by emotional stresses and strains, but by a sort of steel framework of intellectual argument. Embedded in every normal eighteenth-century poem there is a train of thought, which gives it a rigid quality that we do not find or look for in Blake or Shelley. Dryden expressed the critical attitude of the next hundred years when he sneered at Settle, who

> faggoted his notions as they fell,
> And, if they rhim'd and rattl'd, all was well.[1]

What, then, ought Settle to have done? He should have ordered his ideas; he should have thought harder and more consecutively. Of Dryden himself Johnson remarked in his formidable fashion: 'The favourite exercise of his mind was ratiocination'; and, more informally, 'It may be maintained that he was the first who joined argument with poetry.'[2] What Dryden had joined so successfully few eighteenth-century poets cared to put asunder. The favourite device of antithesis is perhaps the most obvious expression of that logical habit of mind which informs eighteenth-century poetry. But, in fact, the ratiocinative manner is universal; it permeates Satire, Epistle, Moral Essay (in all of which we might expect to find it) and even takes control of and shapes the contemporary lyric:

> True as the needle to the Pole,
>   Or as the dial to the Sun;
> Constant as gliding waters roll,
>   Whose swelling tides obey the Moon:
> From ev'ry other charmer free,
> My life and love shall follow thee.

> The lamb the flow'ry thyme devours;
>   The dam the tender kid pursues;
> Sweet Philomel, in shady bowers
>   Of verdant spring, his note renews:
> All follow what they most admire,
> As I pursue my soul's desire.

> Nature must change her beauteous face,
>   And vary as the seasons rise;
> As Winter to the Spring gives place,
>   Summer th' approach of Autumn flies:
> No change in love the seasons bring,
> Love only knows perpetual Spring.

---

[1] *Absalom and Achitophel*, Pt. II, l. 419 f.  See Note P, p. 171.
[2] *Lives*, i. 459, 469.

Devouring time, with stealing pace,
    Makes lofty oaks and cedars bow;
And marble tow'rs, and walls of brass,
    In his rude march he levels low:
But Time, destroying far and wide,
    Love from the soul can ne'er divide.[1]

The writer of those verses is building up a shapely argument,
stanza by stanza; and the argument itself is so normal and
expected that it is easily controlled, and never in any danger of
distorting the shapeliness. There is no urgency in his feelings,
and he has leisure to labour his art; but he feels enough for his
purpose, and metre and metaphor invest his statement with a
finality and largeness that it would not otherwise possess.

Given the intellectual framework, however, the poet was
then free (within reasonable limits) to indulge his wit or fancy.
Johnson, indeed, goes on to say of Dryden that next to ratiocination he delighted in 'wild and daring sallies of sentiment' and
in 'the irregular and excentrick violence of wit'.[2] But 'wit'
was in order only if it was, in Coleridge's rather old-fashioned
phrase, no more than the *drapery* of the poem.[3] The eighteenth-
century critic thought of Fancy or Imagination as a sort of
poetical emanation that flickered upon the surface of the poem,
just as Elizabethan mariners used to see in stormy weather
what they called St. Elmo's fire, 'streaming along with a
sparkeling blaze, halfe the height upon the Maine Mast, and
shooting sometimes from Shroud to Shroud, . . . running sometimes along the Maine-yard to the very end. . . .'[4]

In his 'Thoughts on Poetry and its Varieties' (1859) John
Stuart Mill distinguishes between two kinds of poet:

Whom, then, shall we call poets? Those who are so constituted, that
emotions are the links of association by which their ideas, both sen-
suous and spiritual, are connected together.[5]

Mill proceeds to contrast the 'natural poetry' written by such
poets (e.g. Shelley) with the poetry of 'a cultivated but not

---

[1] 'Song', by Barton Booth, *The Musical Miscellany*, 1729. (Reprinted by D.
Nichol Smith, *The Oxford Book of Eighteenth-Century Verse*, p. 234 f.)
[2] *Lives*, i. 460.
[3] *Biographia Literaria*, ii. 13. The function assigned by Hobbes to Fancy was
mainly decorative or illustrative: 'Fancy begets the ornaments of a Poem' (Spingarn, ii. 59).
[4] Samuel Purchas, *Hakluytus Posthumus or Purchas his Pilgrimes* (1625), IV. 1734.
[5] *English Critical Essays: Nineteenth Century*, ed. Edmund D. Jones, p. 415.

naturally poetic mind' (e.g. Wordsworth). With the Wordsworths feeling waits upon thought; with the Shelleys thought
upon feeling. Readers of Mill may very reasonably refuse to
agree that Wordsworth's poetry is a good example of the work
of 'a cultivated but not naturally poetic mind'; they may,
however, be willing to apply the words to the greater part of
eighteenth-century poetry. In the poetry of Pope and his contemporaries thought does, normally, come first, and thought
remains all-important; it is usually, too, accompanied by feeling
—a warm glow engendered by the thought, and often fanned
into flame by the excitement of composition. For the more
imaginative of the eighteenth-century poets (and Pope must
certainly be included here) we can go on to claim what Johnson claimed for Dryden:

He delighted to tread upon the brink of meaning, where light and
darkness begin to mingle; to approach the precipice of absurdity,
and hover over the abyss of unideal vacancy.[1]

But at its most characteristic eighteenth-century poetry is
rather the poetry of clear, strong statement, packed with meaning: *all* the meaning will not necessarily lie exposed on the
surface, but most of it will, and any further values it has (of
rhythm, texture, allusion) will normally reinforce the surface
meaning.

With Smart's *Song to David* we have obviously passed on to
something much closer to Mill's 'natural' poetry, and in the
songs of Blake we have it at its purest. The attitude of Smart's
contemporaries to the *Song to David* is probably represented
accurately by Mason's comment in a letter to Gray: 'I have
seen his *Song to David*, and from thence conclude him as mad as
ever.'[2] (What Gray thought of the poem is not recorded, but his
opinion was probably more charitable.) The best answer to the
complacent and mediocre Mason is the reply of George II when
someone told him that General Wolfe was mad: 'Oh, he is mad,
is he? Then I wish he would bite some of my other generals.'
The difficulty of the *Song to David* (where it *is* difficult) is largely
the sort of difficulty we encounter when we listen to an excited
man speaking too fast: Smart gobbles his ideas, and his words

---

[1] *Lives*, i. 460. Johnson does not express either approval or disapproval. Hobbes
would certainly have disapproved. He has some strong words about 'the ambitious
obscurity of expressing more than is perfectly conceived' ('Answer to Davenant',
Spingarn, ii. 63).         [2] Gray, *Correspondence*, ii. 802.

have a hit-or-miss urgency to which the eighteenth century was
unaccustomed in polite literature. It is true that the *Song* is far
from being formless, but it is certainly much freer in its associations and much more abrupt in its transitions from one thought
to another than was usual in this period. The contemporary
reader looked in vain for a sustained argument, proceeding
easily and logically from one point to another. Smart appears
to be skimming his ideas as they come to the surface—in fact,
faggoting his notions as they fall.

> Open, and naked of offence,
> Man's made of mercy, soul, and sense;
> God arm'd the snail and wilk;
> Be good to him that pulls thy plough;
> Due food and care, due rest, allow
> For her that yields thee milk.

What was the eighteenth-century reader to make of this?
Where, he must have asked, is the train of thought? It would
have been no answer to him to anticipate John Stuart Mill and
tell him that in this poem thought waited upon feeling. *That*,
he would have replied, is precisely what is the matter with it.
His objections to Smart would have been even more pronounced
if he had been able to read his long *Jubilate Agno*, not published
in Smart's lifetime, and only recently offered to the more
sympathetic readers of the twentieth century. In this strange
effusion there is ample evidence of the imagination, and of a
remarkable sensitiveness to sound and rhythm and the chance
associations which they call up; but what Coleridge called 'the
discriminative and reproductive power' is at times completely
dormant.

Yet if the twentieth-century reader of *Jubilate Agno* is often
defeated by Smart's inconsequential sequences, he is much less
likely to be shocked and repelled by them than Smart's own
contemporaries would have been. In the matter of poetry we
are not, perhaps, all Smarts now, but we have grown accustomed
to approach the individual poem with a willing suspension, or
diminution, of the rational faculties. The modern poet has seen
to that. Coleridge, who can hardly be accused of reading poetry
inattentively (and sometimes even anticipated the modern
highbrow vice of reading it too creatively), had reached this
stage early in the nineteenth century. 'Poetry', he once remarked, 'gives most pleasure when only generally and not

perfectly understood.'[1]  A dangerous statement, no doubt, which could be used by the intellectually lazy to justify mere day-dreaming over the printed page; but Coleridge is surely drawing attention to the irrational element in poetry which cannot be apprehended by the intellect, and only filters through to the reader's consciousness.  In the poetry of the twentieth century the irrational has gained steadily at the expense of the rational.  If we expect in, say, 'The Waste Land' or Dylan Thomas's 'A Winter's Tale' to find the sort of logical structure that supports Gray's *Elegy* we shall be disappointed.  Twentieth-century poetry makes two apparently contradictory demands on the reader: that he should concentrate his attention closely on the poet's words, and that he should be able at the next moment to look away, and allow symbol, sound, and rhythm to float the poet's meaning across his consciousness.  *Across* rather than *into*; for the kind of meaning that the modern poet is often trying to communicate cannot be stated, but must be reflected upon the reader's consciousness by words and symbols that do not so much convey as evoke or suggest the meaning. What is required for the reading of much modern poetry is what often goes into its making: a sort of controlled mind-wandering. Poet and reader must have a mind exceptionally alive to suggestions, and yet be able to resist or discipline those suggestions for the sake (if he is the poet) of passing on as completely and precisely as possible the total poetic experience, or (if he is the reader) of re-creating it from the materials provided by the poet.  Above all, the reader of modern poetry must be able to attain to what Keats called 'Negative Capability'—'that is, when a man is capable of being in uncertainties, mysteries, doubts, without any irritable reaching after fact or reason', when he is capable, indeed, of 'remaining content with half-knowledge'.[2]

The eighteenth century was not so content, and its poets were not encouraged to wander in the unpathed regions of the mind.  They dealt rather with the demonstrable and the palpable, with the known and the expected, with the recurring human situations and feelings and the immemorial habits and activities of mankind.  They moved in a world of certainties, or of uncertainties which had grown so familiar as to have become

[1] *Anima Poetae*, 1895, p. 5.
[2] *The Letters of John Keats*, ed. Maurice Buxton Forman, 1935, p. 72.

in their turn almost certain. In their poetry, as in much else, they preferred to deal with the attainable, and if in so choosing they limited their achievement, it was at least an achievement, and one capable—and surely this is more important than the twentieth century is usually prepared to admit—of being widely understood and enjoyed.

Writing of Pomfret's *Choice*, Johnson observed that it exhibited 'a system of life adapted to common notions and equal to common expectations; such a state as affords plenty and tranquillity, without exclusion of intellectual pleasures'.[1] The words might almost be applied to the world of the eighteenth-century poets, a world of temperate delights and rational pleasures:

> Sound sleep by night; study and ease,
> Together mixt; sweet recreation;
> And innocence, which most does please
> With meditation.

[1] *Lives*, i. 302.

# NOTES

NOTE A, p. 4. The *incredulus odi* attitude of the period may be seen in Rymer's heavy insistence on probability: 'Poetry has no life, nor can have any operation, without *probability*; it may indeed amuse the People, but moves not the Wise' ('Preface to Rapin', Spingarn, ii. 171). A year later, in his Ninth Epistle, Boileau made the uncompromising assertion:

> Rien n'est beau que le vrai: le vrai seul est aimable;
> Il doit régner partout . . . .

NOTE B, p. 14. For earlier indications of the distrust of inspiration and of the tendency to associate it with religious fanaticism, cf. Davenant, 'Preface to *Gondibert*' (Spingarn, ii. 25): 'Yet to such painfull poets some upbraid the want of extemporary fury, or rather *inspiration*, a dangerous word which many have of late successfully us'd; and *inspiration* is a spiritual fitt. . . .' Cf. also Hobbes, 'Answer to Davenant' (Spingarn, ii. 59): '. . . a foolish custome, by which a man, enabled to speak wisely from the principles of nature and his own meditation, loves rather to be thought to speak by inspiration, like a Bagpipe.'

Two books which greatly influenced the contemporary attitude to 'Enthusiasm' were Casaubon's *Treatise concerning Enthusiasme, as it is an Effect of Nature: but is mistaken by many for either Divine Inspiration, or Diabolical Possession* (1665), and Henry More's *Enthusiasmus Triumphatus* (1656). See George Williamson, 'The Restoration Revolt against Enthusiasm', *S.P.* xxx. 571 ff.

NOTE C, p. 23. The neo-classical horror of particularization is seen in a note by John Dennis to his translation of Boileau's Sixth Epistle. In the translation Boileau is made to refer to his 'fortieth rolling year', and Dennis explains in a footnote: 'Boileau, when he writ this, was about six and forty years old; but Poetry admits no odd numbers above nine.' Boileau was, in fact, forty-one. He had avoided the difficulty mentioned by Dennis by referring to his 'neuvième lustre' (Dennis, *Miscellanies in Prose and Verse*, 1693, p. 50 *n.*; cited by Spingarn, ii. 333).

NOTE D, p. 30. To the passage cited from the *Biographia Literaria* Coleridge added a caveat: 'Say not that I am recommending abstractions. . . . Paradoxical as it may sound, one of the essential properties of Geometry is not less essential to dramatic excellence; and Aristotle has accordingly required of the poet an involution of the universal in the individual. The chief differences are, that in Geometry it is the universal truth which is uppermost in the consciousness; in poetry the individual form, in which the truth is clothed.'

NOTE E, p. 67. No one could have been more conscious of his public than Byron, but that consciousness did not inhibit the expression of emotion in his poetry. When Byron was writing, the poet's personal feelings had come to be regarded as the proper stuff of poetry. In his character *as a man*, however, he was often reticent in expressing his feelings. Cf. the account of his behaviour at the exhumation of Shelley's friend Williams: 'Byron's idle talk during the exhumation of Williams's remains did not proceed from want of feeling, but from his anxiety to conceal what he felt from others. . . . He had been taught during his town life, that any exhibition of sympathy or feeling was maudlin and unmanly, and that the appearance of daring and indiffer-ence denoted blood and high breeding' (Trelawny's *Recollections of the Last Days of Shelley and Byron*, ed. E. Dowden, 1906, p. 90).

Note F, p. 70. Even in the correspondence of intimate friends there was usually a reticence in this period that probably surprises the modern reader. In the autumn of 1727 Swift returned to Dublin in poor health and full of anxiety for Stella, who was now 'on the brink of another world'. From Dublin on 12 Oct. he wrote to Pope: 'I have often wished that God Almighty would be so easy to the weakness of mankind, as to let old friends be acquainted in another state; and if I were to write an Utopia for heaven, that would be one of my schemes. This wildness you must allow for, because I am giddy and deaf' (*Correspondence*, ed. F. E. Ball, iii. 442). Such wildness as Swift has permitted himself here would scarcely have seemed to a twentieth-century correspondent, parson or not, to call for any apology.

Note G, p. 77. Isaac Watts puts this distinction clearly in his Dedication of 'A Funeral Poem, On the Death of Thomas Gunston, Esq.': 'Had I designed a complete elegy, madam, on your dearest brother, and intended it for public view, I should have followed the usual forms of poetry, so far at least as to spend some pages in the character and praises of the deceased, and thence have taken occasion to call mankind to complain aloud of the universal and unspeakable loss: but I wrote merely for myself, as a friend of the dead, and to ease my full soul by breathing out my complaints . . .' (Chalmers, xiii. 77).

Note H, p. 82. Wordsworth dismissed the passage as 'vague, bombastic, and senseless', and as showing 'to what a low state of knowledge of the most obvious and important phenomena' poetry had then sunk. Even if the lines justified this charge it is beside the point: Dryden is not trying to write naturalistic poetry. To what, in any case, does Wordsworth take exception? He does not say. He had a proprietary feeling for mountains: was he annoyed that they should be said to nod their drowsy heads? Or was it that birds do not dream, and flowers do not sweat? The passage was very properly admired by Rymer. 'Here', he said, in a passage of unusual insight, 'we have the most raging and watchful passions, Lust and Envy. And these, too, instead of the lustful and the envious, for the greater force and emphasis of the *abstract*.' Those who complain of personifications in eighteenth-century poetry would do well to remember this testimony to their effect on at least one reader.

Note I, p. 85. Boileau would have agreed with Addison. Cf. *L'Art Poétique*, iii. 226 ff., where he writes of those happy names that seem to have been born for poetry:

> Ulysse, Agamemnon, Oreste, Idoménée,
> Hélène, Ménélas, Paris, Hector, Énée.
> Oh! le plaisant projet d'un poète ignorant,
> Qui de tant de héros va choisir Childebrand!

D'un seul nom quelquefois le son dur ou bizarre
Rend un poème entier ou burlesque ou barbare.

NOTE J, p. 91. Warburton's sneer at Francis Peck the antiquary is typical of the attitude of many eighteenth-century readers: '. . . he is at present busy upon a collection of all our ancient English ballads; which, I understand, he intends to give with notes and emendations. With all this he thinks he is serving the world. May it always be thus served! its neglect of merit, its ingratitude, and universal corruption, deserving no other devotees' (J. Nichols, *Literary Illustrations*, ii. 28).

NOTE K, p. 103. Tickell was not alone in this belief. In 1766 Dr. J. Gregory wrote to the poet Beattie: 'It is a sentiment that very universally prevails, that poetry is a light kind of reading, which one takes up only for a little amusement, and that therefore it should be so perspicuous as not to require a second reading. This sentiment would bear hard on some of your best things, and on all Gray's except his "Churchyard Elegy", which, he told me, with a good deal of acrimony, owed its popularity entirely to the subject, and that the public would have received it as well if it had been written in prose' (Sir William Forbes, *Life of James Beattie*, 1824, p. 44).

NOTE L, p. 111. St. Évremond had expressed the same opinion long before Beattie. 'A tale of woods, rivers, meadows, fields, and gardens, makes but a very languishing impression upon us, unless their beauties be wholly new: but what concerns Humanity, its inclinations, tendernesses, and affections, finds something in the innermost recesses of our souls prepar'd to receive it: the same nature produces and receives 'em, and they are easily transfus'd from the actors to the spectators' (*The Works of Monsieur St. Evremond, Made English . . . .* The Second Edition, 1728, ii. 61).

NOTE M, p. 138. There were certain recognized openings for decorative effect. Boileau advises the epic poet to be 'vif et pressé' in his narrative passages, but to let himself go on the descriptions:

Soyez riche et pompeux dans vos descriptions:
C'est là qu'il faut des vers étaler l'élégance.

For an English poet, being 'riche et pompeux' usually meant writing in the style of Milton, and that meant writing in blank verse. Johnson certainly expressed the normal opinion about blank verse when he asserted that it could only support itself with the help of rhetorical devices. 'If blank verse be not tumid and gorgeous, it is crippled prose' (*Lives*, ii. 319 f.). It is no answer to Johnson to cite Lear's

Pray, do not mock me:
I am a very foolish fond old man,
Fourscore and upward; not an hour more nor less . . .

or the fine close of Wordsworth's 'Michael':

Among the rocks
He went, and still looked up to sun and cloud,
And listened to the wind . . . .

No one has ever doubted that there can be short *passages* of entire simplicity in blank verse. The problem, however, remains: can blank verse on a consistently subdued level be tolerated all the way through a play or a long poem? Even in his 'Michael' Wordsworth was sometimes driven to the sort of heightening that Johnson had in mind; e.g. ll. 110 ff. in which he describes the cottage chimney 'with huge and black projection overbrowed', where hung a lamp, 'an aged utensil', the 'surviving comrade of uncounted hours'.

NOTE N, p. 141. To Boileau, writing in 1674, the pagan deities offered the poet some of his noblest opportunities:

> Tout prend un corps, une âme, un esprit, un visage.
> Chaque vertu devient une divinité:
> Minerve est la prudence, et Vénus la beauté.
> Ce n'est plus la vapeur qui produit le tonnerre,
> C'est Jupiter armé pour effrayer la terre . . . .

Without such ornaments, Boileau feels, 'la poésie est morte' (*L'Art Poétique*, iii. 150 ff.). In course of time the very opposite came to be true, and the god became a gorgon to the poem in which he appeared.

NOTE O, p. 154. Further excursions into unfamiliar regions, in which the eighteenth-century poet threw off his habitual responsibilities to the reader, may be found in such pieces as Young's 'Paraphrase on Part of the Book of Job', Gray's Norse and Welsh odes, Francis Fawkes's translations of Gawin Douglas, the numerous imitations of English and Scots ballads (e.g. by William Hamilton of Bangour, Mallet, Shenstone, Mickle, Goldsmith, Chatterton, Cowper), and such popular songs as Gay's 'Sweet William's Farewell to Black-Ey'd Susan' or Carey's 'Sally in our Alley', with their conscious but not too-sophisticated simplicity. In these and other experiments in translation and imitation the poet is not speaking altogether with the voice of his own century; he is trying to recapture the effect of a poetry that may be very different from that of his own age. Whether his readers approve or disapprove of the results, they will judge the poet mainly by those of his works that are in the contemporary poetical idiom. Success in his imitations may add to his reputation; failure will not seriously detract from it. Had Chatterton first made a name for himself by writing Pastorals and Epistles in the modern style, and *then* proceeded quite openly to write 'Ælla', 'The Bristowe Tragedie', and 'An Excelente Balade of Charitie' as professed imitations, he might have had a greater reputation among his contemporaries.

NOTE P, p. 162. Dryden gives a reasoned statement of his objections to writers like Settle in *Notes and Observations on the Empress of Morocco* (1674). 'Some who are pleased with the bare sound of verse, or the rumbling of robustious nonsense, will be apt to think Mr. Settle too severely handled in this pamphlet. . . . I am not ignorant that his admirers, who most commonly are women, will resent this very ill; and some little friends of his, who are smatterers in poetry, will be ready for most of his gross errors to use that mistaken plea of *poetica licentia*, which words fools are apt to use for the palliating the most absurd nonsense in any poem. I cannot find when poets had liberty, from any authority, to write nonsense, more than any other men. Nor is that plea of *poetica licentia* used as a subterfuge by any but weak professors of that art, who are commonly given over to a mist of fancy, a buzzing of invention, and a sound of something like sense, and have no use of judgment. They never think thoroughly, but the best of their thoughts are like those we have in dreams, imperfect; which though perhaps we are often pleased with sleeping, we blush at waking. . . . Men that are given over to fancy only, are little better than madmen. . . . Their heads are continually hot, and they have the same elevation of fancy sober, which men of sense have when they drink' (*Works*, ed. Sir Walter Scott, xv. 409 f.).

## ADDITIONAL NOTES TO THE THIRD IMPRESSION

pp. 48–9. Professor Richard D. Altick has drawn my attention to the fact that the figures I originally quoted from Lord Jeffrey, viz. 300,000 and 30,000, were in fact the figures given by him when he revised his review for republication in a collected edition in 1844. The alteration almost certainly indicates that the reading public had grown considerably in the interval.

p. 161. In an interesting article, 'Logical Structure in Eighteenth-Century Poetry' (*Philological Quarterly*, xxxi, No. 3, July 1952, pp. 315–36), Mr. D. J. Greene takes exception to a statement of mine that 'The poetry written in England from the time of Dryden had been characterized . . . by a sound logical structure'. Although he seems to me to have been carried too far by the ardour of his pursuit in the opposite direction, I now see that the phrase 'logical structure' is misleading, and I have withdrawn it. If Mr. Greene had pondered what I say on pp. 109–10 he would have seen that I do not maintain that eighteenth-century poetry often lived up to Shaftesbury's demand that 'every several part or portion [should fit] its proper place so exactly that the least transposition would be impracticable'. What I still wish to maintain is that the eighteenth-century poet normally proceeded from point to point, if not logically, at any rate on the plane of reasonable discourse, that an argument, however discursive, usually emerges, and that his readers felt reassured when he effected his transitions from one point to another at least with a show of reason. Quoting the poem printed on pp. 162–3, Mr. Greene remarks: 'But where, we ask after reading the poem, *is* the argument? . . . The poem leads to no conclusion at all. It is a reiterated statement that the poet is in love, and will remain in love.' I am sorry that poor Barton Booth should be brought blinking back into a limelight that neither he nor his poem can easily face. But the argument, such as it is, is surely not hard to find: (1) 'As the needle is true to the pole etc. . . . so am I true and constant to you. (2) As the lamb . . . kid . . . nightingale follow what they like best, so I pursue you, my soul's desire. (3) Although the face of Nature changes with the seasons, the seasons bring no change to my love for you. (4) Not time itself, which changes almost all things, can destroy my love for you.' This, I will agree, is not a logical structure: but it is surely an argument, i.e. 'a connected series of statements or reasons intended to establish a position' (*O.E.D.*).

# INDEX

Minor references and references to the Notes (pp. 168–72) are omitted